What people have said about
the original Lincoln campaign biography of 1860:

"most authoritative and influential"

—New York Times

"a charming readable story having documents and dignity ..."
about this fabulous human figure [Abraham Lincoln]"

—Carl Sandburg
Pulitzer Prize Historian

"Of greater lasting merit ... based on an extensive autobiographical
sketch that Lincoln gave [to John Locke Scripps]"

—David Herbert Donald
Pulitzer Prize Historian
Harvard University

VOTE LINCOLN!

Abraham Lincoln for President, 1860
This celebrated poster suggests surprising youthfulness.
(He was 51 years old. His iconic beard came later still.)

VOTE LINCOLN!

The Presidential Campaign Biography
of
Abraham Lincoln, 1860

Restored & Annotated

by
John Locke Scripps
and
Abraham Lincoln

Illustrated with Historic Images

Restored & Annotated by
David W. Bradford
Editor

Expanded Edition

Boston Hill Press

Boston Hill Press
Editorial Office
P.O. Box 215583
Town & Country Post Office
Sacramento, CA 95821

Printed in the United States of America.
Printed & Distributed by
Lightning Source, Inc. (LSI)
La Vergne, TN 37086

A version of this expanded edition was published in hardcover.
Publisher's Cataloging-in-Publication Data for the hardcover edition is:
Scripps, J. L. (John Locke), 1818-1866.
Vote Lincoln! the presidential campaign biography of Abraham Lincoln, 1860;
restored and annotated / John Locke Scripps, Abraham Lincoln.
Edited by David W. Bradford. Expanded edition.
p. cm.
Includes bibliographical references and index.
1. Lincoln, Abraham, 1809-1865—Political career before 1861.
2. Presidents—United States—Biography.   3. United States—Politics and govern-
ment—Civil War, 1861-1865. 4. Presidents—United States—Election—1860.
5. Lincoln, Abraham, 1809-1865—Oratory.
I. Lincoln, Abraham, 1809-1865. II. Title.
III. Title: Life of Abraham Lincoln.
E457.3 .S429 2010
973.7092 [B]
Library of Congress Catalog No. 2010900185

ISBN-13: 978-0-9787992-4-3 (hardcover)
ISBN-13: 978-0-9787992-5-0 (softcover)

New Contents[1]

Life of Abraham Lincoln[2]

---

[1] Contents differ from the original book of 1860, which had no prefatory or end matter. The preface, introduction, epilogue, etc., are modern additions.

[2] Original title of the book in 1860.

[3] The 1860 text skips from Chapter Six to Chapter Eight. This may be only a typographical error, but the publishers also shortened the book to save costs.

Abraham Lincoln
Springfield, Illinois
June 1860
Photograph by Alexander Hesler.

Preface to the Restored Editions

For over a century, partisans have anointed their favorite political candidates as the "next Abraham Lincoln." This is exceptionally high praise. In life and in death, Abraham Lincoln achieved worldwide acclaim as not only a great American president, but as a moral icon. He fulfilled a universal prophecy of mankind: A noble warriorking sacrificed his life to save his people from tyranny.

However, what did Abraham Lincoln say about *himself* when he was the newcomer? A long-forgotten book provides a glimpse. In June 1860, Mr. Lincoln secretly helped write his own campaign biography. His coauthor, John Locke Scripps, polished and expanded it into a bestseller that is discreetly Lincoln on Lincoln.

In some ways, the book presents the candidate in a remarkably modern fashion. He defends his antiwar past;[1] critiques the Supreme Court on civil liberties; touts "Whig" policies, i.e., big government programs; sides proudly with everyday working people; and favors high-wage U.S. industries over foreign-made products.[2]

Nonetheless, Abraham Lincoln's campaign biography is a unique product of his time, not ours. Within its pages, an eternal legend comes to life: From a troubled childhood of tragic loss and grinding poverty, a small boy rises to become a mighty crusader for justice. This cherished icon endures, undimmed across the ages.

---

[1] He opposed the U.S. invasion of Mexico in the late 1840s. See Chapter Six.

[2] See New Appendix B for more details about his campaign platform.

Mr. Lincoln's book also frankly discusses the central issue of *his* day. The candidate unflinchingly denounces slavery, then a powerful and aggressive force. Doggedly, Mr. Lincoln warns of slavery's threat to the freedom of *all* Americans.

Most importantly, he argues that slavery is always morally wrong. Nothing justifies the then enslavement of black people. He dismisses both tradition and prejudice, including his own, as illegitimate rationalizations.[1] Tyranny, brutality, depravity—all make slavery morally wrong.

His moralizing, though, evoked outrage from many. Some howled that slavery was morally *good*. Others swore vile threats. Even supposed statesmen rebuked him. Mr. Lincoln's rival for the presidency, Stephen Douglas, blamed *him* for the commotion and huffed that slavery was about "public policy," not morality. (Mr. Douglas was a former ally of slaveholders and routinely spouted racial slurs.)

Mr. Lincoln faults his critics for their lax ways. "If slavery is not wrong," he later added, "nothing is wrong," i.e., slavery corrupts everything and everyone. Nevertheless, no major presidential candidate ever again appealed to morality with such passion.

Mr. Lincoln would have been undaunted. As he reminds us in his book, most politicians are not long remembered after their "poor tongues" are stilled. He believes instead in a more enduring saga— the eternal struggle between right and wrong. "They are the two principles that have stood face to face from the beginning of time," Mr. Lincoln observes, "and will ever continue to struggle."

As usual, Abraham Lincoln has the last word.

David W. Bradford, Editor
Lincoln Bicentennial Year, 2009

---

[1] He deflects race-baiting in an unorthodox manner. See page 166.

About this Expanded Edition

This is a revised and expanded edition of *Vote Lincoln! The Presidential Campaign Biography of Abraham Lincoln, 1860; Restored and Annotated.* The first restored edition was published in year 2009; this expanded edition makes further refinements, e.g., more illustrations and commentary. The designation "New" in some section titles, e.g., "New Epilogue," refers to modern material not in the original book of 1860. Other modern features include the preface and introduction. These modern sections debut in the first restored edition and reappear here with only modest revision. — The Editor

LINCOLN'S HOME IN SPRINGFIELD, ILLINOIS.

LIFE

OF

ABRAHAM LINCOLN.

CHAPTER I.

EARLY LIFE.

His Ancestors—His Grandfather Murdered by Indians—His Parents—An Only Child—Adverse Circumstances—Western Schools Fifty Years Ago—Removal to Indiana—Work in the Forest—Letter-Writer for the Neighborhood—The First Great Sorrow—Character of his Mother—Reading the Scriptures—Self-Educated—First Books—Interesting Incident of Boyhood—Early Western Preachers.

IT is not known at what period the ancestors of Abraham Lincoln came to America. The first account that has been obtained of them dates back about one hundred and fifty years, at which time they were living in Berks County, Pennsylvania, and were members of the Society of Friends. Whence or when they came to that region is not known.

About the middle of the last century, the great-grandfather of Abraham Lincoln removed from Berks County, Pennsylvania, to Rockingham County, Virginia. There Abraham Lincoln, the grandfather, and Thomas Lincoln, the father of the subject of this sketch, were born. Abraham, the grandfather, had four brothers—Isaac, Jacob, John, and Thomas—descendants of whom are now living in Virginia, North Carolina, Kentucky, Tennessee, and Missouri. Abraham removed to Kentucky about the year 1780, and four years thereafter, while engaged in opening a farm, he was surprised and killed by Indians; leaving a widow, three sons, and two daughters. The eldest son, Mordecai, remained in Kentucky until late in life, when he removed to Hancock County, Illinois, where he shortly afterward died, and where his descendants still live. The second son, Josiah, settled many years ago on Blue River, in Harrison County, Indiana. The eldest daughter, Mary, was married to Ralph Crume, and some of her descendants are now living in Breckenridge County, Kentucky. The second daughter, Nancy, was married to William Brumfield, and her descendants are supposed to be living in Kentucky.

Thomas, the youngest son, and father of the subject of this sketch, by the death of his father and the very narrow circumstances of his mother, was thrown upon his own resources while yet a child. Traveling from neighborhood to neighborhood, working wherever he could find employment, he grew up literally without education. He finally settled in Hardin County, where, in 1806, he was married to Nancy Hanks, whose family had also come from Virginia. The fruits of this union were a daughter and two sons. One of the latter died in infancy; the daughter died later in life, having been married, but leaving no issue. The sole survivor is the subject of this sketch.

Abraham Lincoln was born in Hardin County, Kentucky, February 12th, 1809. It would be difficult to conceive of more unpromising circumstances than those under which he was ushered into life. His parents were poor and uneducated. They were under the social ban which the presence of slavery always entails upon poverty. Their very limited means and the low grade of the neighboring schools, precluded the expectation of conferring upon their children the advantages of even a common English education. The present inhabitants of the Western States can have but a faint idea of the schools which fifty years ago constituted the only means of education accessible to the poorer classes. The teachers were, for the most part, ignorant, uncultivated men, rough of speech, uncouth in manners, and rarely competent to teach beyond the simplest rudiments of learning—"spelling, reading, writing," and sometimes a very little arithmetic. The books of study then in vogue, would not now be tolerated in schools of the lowest grade. The school-house, constructed of logs, floorless, windowless, and without inclosure, was in admirable harmony with teacher, text-books, and the mode of imparting instruction.

In his seventh year, Abraham was sent for short periods to two of these schools, and while attending them progressed so far as to learn to write. For this acquirement he manifested a great fondness. It was his custom to form letters, to write words and sen-

The Lincoln Biography, 1860
It was then a 32-page pamphlet of dense small print.
This is a reduced facsimile of the first page.

A Modern Note About Format

Regrettably, forgotten allusions, highly condensed passages, and Victorian-era rhetoric now obscure the original 1860 text. To restore readability, this is a changed edition. It has a modern preface, glossary, introduction, epilogue, and appendices—all not in the original book. Clarifying annotation is [in brackets]; new essays and other supplemental material in text boxes. Footnotes provide further elaboration, as do historic images placed in context. (The 1860 book lacked illustrations.) Grammar, punctuation, and layout are also updated.

Nevertheless, historical terminology requires careful note. *Slavery* referred to the forced unpaid labor of captive human beings. *Free labor* meant *paid* workers with constitutional rights and freedom. *Free North* or *Free States* referred to Northern States which banned slavery; *slave South*, to Southern States where the institution was legal.

Also, the political parties of 1860 were unique. The *Democratic Party of 1860* opposed government intervention in the economy and society. The party was racist and recently allied with slaveholders.

The *Republican Party of 1860* was antislavery. It favored government assistance to workers and farmers, and was based in States of the Free North, stretching from New England to the Pacific Coast.

Finally, the distinction between *States* and *Territories* was important.[1] In 1860, most *States* were in the East. The American West was mostly divided into *Territories,* with too few people yet for statehood, and no votes in national elections. How and when the Western *Territories* became *States,* i.e., could vote *for* slavery, or *for* freedom, determined future control of Congress and the presidency of the United States.

---

[1] Both terms are capitalized in this restored text, as per the practice of 1860.

Adapted from T.A. Dodge, *Our Civil War,* 1911

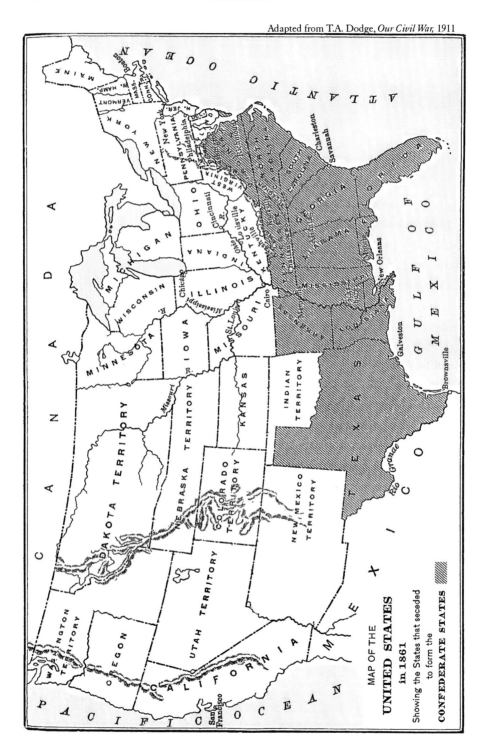

MAP OF THE
UNITED STATES
in 1861
Showing the States that seceded
to form the
CONFEDERATE STATES

Editor's Introduction

The U.S. presidential election of November 1860 was one of the most dramatic ever conducted—the momentous possibility of civil war loomed large. However, the presidential candidates, including Abraham Lincoln, carefully avoided broaching the unspoken taboo.

Rather, on the surface, the presidential election of 1860 was a familiar one, characterized by colorful conventions; artful slogans; partisan media; instantaneous communication;[1] and last, but not least, the promotion of carefully crafted biographies into national bestsellers.

And no candidate was as skilled in these modern campaign techniques as Abraham Lincoln.

Newcomer – Nevertheless, in the summer of 1860, on the eve of the fall campaign, Mr. Lincoln was still not a household name for many Americans. He was a dark-horse nominee for president, having unexpectedly overtaken a popular front-runner. By contrast, Stephen Douglas, the foremost opponent in the coming election, was a much discussed celebrity. (In the preceding decade, Mr. Douglas embraced a series of controversial positions on slavery—on *both* sides of the debate.)

This imbalance in name recognition created enormous demand for information about the newcomer. During the ensuing campaign of 1860, publishers hurriedly issued no less than eighteen authorized and unauthorized biographies about Abraham Lincoln. The candidate himself covertly assisted several of their authors, including William Dean Howells, D. W. Bartlett, and John Locke Scripps.

---

[1] The electric telegraph entered service in 1844, allowing newspapers to print several editions per day of transcontinental news.

Confidence
August 13, 1860

On the eve of the autumn presidential campaign, Abraham Lincoln relaxes in his office in Springfield, Illinois. He sports a summer tan.

Library of Congress

However, the book by John Locke Scripps must be considered the official *Presidential Campaign Biography of Abraham Lincoln, 1860,* and is the basis of this revival. Mr. Lincoln was a friend of Mr. Scripps; secretly wrote for him a partial manuscript (reprinted in New Appendix A); and had tight editorial control over the project.[1] Mr. Scripps polished and greatly expanded the manuscript, but the final book was as much the candidate's as it was the biographer's.

In addition, the antislavery movement financed and distributed the book. Two allied publishers, Mr. Scripps's Chicago *Press and Tribune* and Horace Greeley's New York *Tribune,*[2] issued related editions, and political activists promoted the book throughout America. With such certain backing, the campaign biography had a first printing of one-million copies.[3]

---

[1] He insisted on many deletions. Grace Locke Scripps Dyche, ed., *The First Published Life of Abraham Lincoln,* (Detroit: Cranebrook Press, 1900), p. 5.

[2] Mr. Greeley is also famous for uttering, "Go West, young man, go West!"

[3] Horace White to Abraham Lincoln, 27 June 1860, Abraham Lincoln Papers at the Library of Congress; Carl Sandburg, *Abraham Lincoln: The Prairie Years and the War Years* (New York: Harcourt, Brace Jovanovich, 1974), p. 179. Many copies were likely distributed free as campaign handouts. The cash price was as low as 2 to 5 cents each (about 44 cents to $1.10 in modern dollars).

The quality of the writing was also noteworthy, epitomizing the modern genre of campaign biography, i.e., humble beginnings that lead to national greatness. Carl Sandburg, a Pulitzer Prize biographer, praised the book as a "charming readable story having documents and dignity."[1]

The Arena – Abraham Lincoln published his biography in July 1860, on the eve of an exceptionally harsh political campaign. Three major opponents for the presidency confronted him in that November's *general* election, including not only Stephen Douglas of Illinois, but two favorite sons of the South, John C. Breckenridge and John Bell. The rivals vehemently disparaged Mr. Lincoln—the electric telegraph, like the Internet today, instantly transmitted their disagreements to a transcontinental nation.

The grounds for contention were strikingly broad. The four presidential nominees held vastly different opinions about foreign policy, the economy, and cultural issues. (An iconoclast in a chauvinist era,

John Locke Scripps (1818-66)
Antislavery Newspaperman
Chicago, Illinois

A founder of what became the Chicago Tribune, *he was a sponsor, editor, and coauthor of Mr. Lincoln's campaign biography.*

Dyche, 1900

---

[1] Sandburg, p. 179.

Horace Greeley (1805-76)
Antislavery Newspaperman
New York City

He was America's foremost publisher,
and a sponsor of Mr. Lincoln's cam-
paign biography.

Stephenson, 1921

Mr. Lincoln had a lifelong empathy for the condition of women. His mother, sister, and first love, Ann Rutledge, had all died tragically.)[1]

However, one issue dominated all others: slavery. Nearly 4-million people of African descent—more than ten percent of *all* Americans—were held in a grueling captivity, mostly as agricultural workers in the Southern States. Slavery's *existence*, though, was *not* the main dispute; most people long tolerated a "peculiar institution" that seemed distant and remote, i.e., confined to the Deep South.

Rather, slavery's *expansion,* or threat thereof, deeply agitated the nation. Decades of peaceful coexistence and voluntary restraint were at end. Proslavery militants agitated to seize the vast new lands of the American West; some slaveholders predicted an "empire of slavery."

Moreover, allies of slavery dominated the federal government and routed their critics. In the general election of 1860, the four presidential nominees echoed this dynamic. Only Abraham Lincoln flatly opposed slavery's expansion. His three rivals hedged, were silent, or openly endorsed slavery.

The Crisis – By the eve of the 1860 campaign, all federal limits on domestic slavery had ceased. Many state laws still forbade slavery, but all were in the Free North. The latter was a patchwork quilt of farming

---

[1]   His mother died of disease, when he was 9 years old; his sister perished in childbirth, when he was 18; his first love succumbed to fever, when he was 26.

Frederick Douglass (1818-95)
Ex-Slave & Civil Rights Leader
Rochester, New York

He warned that slavery threatened all
Americans, regardless of skin color.

National Archives

and industrial States stretching from New England westward. Surprisingly, though, this last bastion of freedom was also under threat.

As early as 1853, Frederick Douglass, an antislavery activist and an ex-slave, warned about a risk to *all* Americans.[1] For slaves no longer worked only in Southern agriculture. They also toiled in factories, construction sites, and shipyards as far North as Maryland. This *industrial* slavery competed with companies using "free" labor, i.e., *paid* workers with personal freedom. The danger was clear: Slave companies could underprice and eliminate firms paying decent wages.

Slave labor must destroy free labor, some observers concluded.

This dreaded dynamic also threatened family farming, then the occupation of most Americans. The threat was unexpected, as Conegress long reserved most new lands for family farms. In 1857, the Supreme Court suddenly ended restrictions on slavery in the Far West and Great Plains. New slave plantations *could* displace family farms.

Concerned voters flocked to a new political movement, one seeking to preserve the freedoms won by the American Revolution of 1776. Eventually called *Republicans*, a slate of antislavery candidates quick-

---

[1] In 1853, Mr. Douglass warned that "White men are becoming house-servants, cooks, and stewards, common laborers, and flunkeys ... This fact proves that if we [colored people] cannot rise to the whites, the whites can fall to us."

ly won elections in the Northern States. By early 1860, U.S. Senator William Seward of New York was their national leader.

However, in a major upset, Abraham Lincoln, a self-taught lawyer from frontier Illinois, defeated the urbane Mr. Seward for the antislavery nomination for president. The rivals, though, quickly closed ranks. The losing Mr. Seward campaigned hard for Mr. Lincoln in the general election of 1860 and urged his supporters to do likewise.[1]

The Opponent – In the November election, Mr. Lincoln's main opponent, Stephen Douglas, was a longtime nemesis, dating back decades to state politics in Illinois. Mr. Douglas had since become one of the most powerful politicians in America, and well known as a no-holds-barred operative. His views on slavery were suspect: In 1854, Senator Douglas dragged his Democratic Party into a controversial alliance with Southern slaveholders, and temporarily won their support.

However, in 1860, Stephen Douglas often presented himself as a friend of the *antislavery* movement. His eleventh-hour conversion was not mysterious. Public opinion in the Northern States had hardened against slavery, and the region's "swing States" were needed to win the presidency. The adaptable Mr. Douglas downplayed his former alliance with the slave South and unabashedly campaigned for the same Northern votes sought by Mr. Lincoln. (The Southern States

William Seward (1801-72)
U.S. Senator, R-N.Y., 1849-61

In a major upset, Abraham Lincoln defeated him for the antislavery nomination for President.

Library of Congress

---

[1] Presidential elections are a two-step process. Candidates compete in the general election only after securing the nomination of their political party.

Stephen Douglas (1813-61)
U.S. Senator, D-Ill., 1847-61

He ran against Mr. Lincoln in the general election for the presidency. Poster by Currier & Ives, July 1860.

Library of Congress

disowned the national parties and opted for third-party candidates John C. Breckenridge of Kentucky and John Bell of Tennessee.)

The Message – Abraham Lincoln's campaign biography was likely his only major presentation during the general election campaign.[1] He largely avoided making other substantive statements in the fall of 1860. As such, his biography attracted much attention during the campaign and its aftermath, i.e., the beginning of the American Civil War.

Mr. Lincoln benefited greatly from the scrutiny. His book recounts decades of colorful political activity and excerpts his best speeches. The narrative forcefully reiterates his longstanding attack on slavery as a threat to the freedom of *all* Americans, not just the slaves.

In particular, Mr. Lincoln accuses his main opponent, Stephen Douglas, of being a ringleader of a conspiracy to spread slavery throughout the nation. In the decade before 1860, the conspirators allegedly created a nightmarish system: Federal law *promoted* slavery, rather than restricted it. Moreover, Mr. Lincoln predicts that Mr. Douglas and his cohorts will soon use the federal government to overturn laws of Free States, and force slavery upon unwilling communities.

Others had long warned of similar plots, but Mr. Lincoln's charge was bolstered by a deep economic recession then underway in the United States. Called the "Panic of 1857," financial scandals destroyed

---

[1] He aided a few other authors, but their books were not as influential.

the livelihoods of many farmers, workers, and businessmen. There was no recovery before the presidential campaign of 1860.

Although the relationship between slavery and the recession was unclear, the "Panic of 1857" made people seriously consider slavery's potential harm to *white* people, and not just the black slaves. At the very least, a suspect federal government opposed economic relief and blocked grants of public land to hungry farmers.

Hence, voters were receptive to Mr. Lincoln's book. In it, he proposes to immediately halt the territorial expansion of *new* slavery, and to gradually phase out *existing* slavery. His official campaign platform, published separately, facilitates transition to a more modern economy. He would distribute land to family farmers; construct major public works, e.g., a transcontinental railroad; and protect American jobs by heavily taxing foreign-made products.[1]

As such, both enslaved blacks *and* free white people would benefit from Mr. Lincoln's policies. He restricts slavery *and* bolsters the free economy. This he believes is the path to slavery's ultimate end.

Silence – However, his campaign biography is also notable for what it does *not* contain. He emphatically rejects using force to settle the slavery dispute and offers no quick solutions. Mr. Lincoln's policies might require decades, if ever, to eradicate slavery.

His sincerity is not at issue. Rather, a lifelong pacifism limits his actions.[2] He only bans slavery from where it is not yet firmly established, i.e., in the frontier lands of the American West. Fearing violent resistance, he would *not* abolish existing slavery in the Southern States. Instead, he awaits a voluntary end at some unspecified future date.

Mr. Lincoln views this delay as the necessary price of nonviolence. He would even continue longstanding federal guarantees to slaveholders, including returning escaped slaves to captivity. However, such ancient "compromise" dismayed many of his own supporters and was increasingly ineffective at keeping the peace. (Armed clashes had already erupted in Kansas and Virginia.)

---

[1] See New Appendix B for details about Mr. Lincoln's campaign platform.
[2] See Chapters Three and Six for his antihero, antiwar past.

Third-Party Candidates, 1860

John C. Breckinridge of Kentucky (above left) boasted slavery was "really profitable" and was the nominee of the Southern Democratic Party. John Bell of Tennessee (above right) led a nebulous Constitutional Union Party that had no stated policy on slavery. Posters by Currier & Ives, 1860.

Indeed, Mr. Lincoln omits what he might do if violence were to spread. Instead, he predicts a peaceful future, when slaveholders will voluntarily end the system that enriches them. In short, Mr. Lincoln wishes away his own warning of 1858, only two years earlier: A "house divided," half slave and half free, could not stand.

As such, during the presidential campaign of 1860, many disbelieved Mr. Lincoln's avowed restraint. They thought he was merely posturing, trying to be all things to all people. How could an antislavery crusader *not* free the slaves?

Yet, even after winning the presidency, and the start of bloody battles with proslavery rebels, Mr. Lincoln opposed forcibly freeing the slaves. He sternly rebuked both congressmen and military commanders who sought to do otherwise.

Instead, President Lincoln initially viewed the Civil War as a struggle to suppress insurrection, not slavery. He fought rebels not because they were proslavery, but because they violated the laws of the United States and attacked its government. He would not disturb those slaveholders who did not engage in such violence.

Campaign Poster, 1860

The new president still viewed slavery as an issue to be resolved politically, and separately from the war. He claimed this restraint would reassure slaveholders in Border States, e.g., his native Kentucky, and thereby reduce violence. His former acquaintances—including his wife's relatives—were supposedly less bellicose and would not join the "Confederate" war against the United States.

In other words, to the surprise of many, the new president honored the promise of his campaign biography: He would not use force to settle the dispute over slavery. His eclectic book was sincere. As a candidate in 1860, he was, just as he claimed, an anguished moderate, unable to agree with either extreme of the slavery debate.

As for the savage warfare that began in early 1861, President Lincoln initially deferred to his generals. His biography admitted little military experience, and he constrained himself accordingly. That modesty, though, proved disastrous as inept commanders wandered into a series of calamitous defeats. (Mr. Lincoln's overtures to the Border States availed him little. Many residents therein, including several of his in-laws, joined the proslavery rebellion.)

Guilt-ridden, the novice president confronted a painful contradiction: He hesitated to destroy a "slave power" that he himself branded as dangerous and immoral. "We must free the slaves," he belatedly moaned in 1862, "or be ourselves subdued."[1]

Only after armed invasion by proslavery forces into the Free North —threatening Philadelphia, Washington, and New York—did the legendary Abraham Lincoln of the Civil War finally appear. He became everything that his campaign biography said he could never be: a determined commander in chief and the great emancipator of slaves. (Mr. Lincoln was the last sitting American president to be an active battlefield commander, and to face enemy bullets.)[2]

How Abraham Lincoln, the descendant of Quakers, traversed the great distance between his pacifist biography and military victory in the Civil War is beyond the scope of this book. Indeed, much of that transformation remains a mystery. Like many other campaign biographies, Mr. Lincoln's book of 1860 only provides a sketch of the *man* that he had been before his candidacy. What kind of *president* he would be, remains the subject of future books by others.

Nevertheless, Mr. Lincoln's campaign biography continues to distinguish itself as among the best of its genre. Despite the limits of hard-nosed politics, it offers an unusual measure of truth, making it not only valuable history, but an enduring moral beacon. As such, both book and message live on: Abraham Lincoln's noble crusade against slavery is the unspoken backdrop for all subsequent campaigns to be president of the United States.

D. W. B.

---

[1]   Lord Charnwood, *Abraham Lincoln* (New York: Henry Holt, 1917), p. 318.

[2]   In 1862, he directed an assault on Norfolk, Virginia. In 1864, rebels returned the favor, firing on him near Washington, D.C. Sandburg, pp. 294-95, 528-29.

New Glossary of Names

Well before he ran for president, Abraham Lincoln's life was already a great human drama, marked by foreshadowing and a memorable Shakespearean cast. Characters of those early years include:

Childhood
Thomas Lincoln and Nancy Hanks – Impoverished parents. Mother dies of disease when her son is only nine years old.
Sarah Lincoln – Only sister who also perishes tragically young.
Sarah Bush Johnston – Kindly stepmother who encourages reading.

Working Youth
Dennis Offutt – Businessman who hires young Abraham Lincoln to man a flatboat to New Orleans—700 miles into the dark heart of slavery.
John Hanks – Cousin who joins the flatboat crew.
John Calhoun – A land surveyor who offers first professional job, but who later becomes a proslavery opponent.
John T. Stuart – Small-town attorney who encourages study of the law.
Mary Todd – Well-to-do young woman who believes in the struggling novice Mr. Lincoln, and defies her family to marry him.

Statesman
Stephen A. Douglas – Early nemesis and future rival for the presidency.
Henry Clay and Daniel Webster – Political role models and presidential contenders of the doomed Whig Party. They seek peaceful compromise on slavery, but lose to growing extremism.
U.S. President James Polk – Militarist whose cohorts smear the antiwar Congressman Lincoln, ending his first political career at age 40.
James A. Shields – Erratic foe who once sought a duel to the death.
Lyman Trumbull – Opponent who defects to the antislavery cause. Mr. Lincoln joins forces with him, sparking a political revolution.

- [Start of 1860 text.] -

LIFE

OF

ABRAHAM LINCOLN[1]

---

[1]   Original title of the book in 1860.

Opposite Page: The Kentucky wilderness of Abraham Lincoln's childhood.
As a small boy, he nearly drowned in the swift Knob Creek (foreground).

Chapter One
Early Life

His Ancestors—His Grandfather Murdered by Indians—His Parents—An Only Child—Adverse Circumstances—Western Schools Fifty Years Ago—Removal to Indiana—Work in the Forest—Letter Writer for the Neighborhood —The First Great Sorrow—Character of his Mother—Reading the Scriptures—Self-Educated—First Books—Interesting Incident of Boyhood—Early Western Preachers.

I T is not known [at the time of this writing in 1860] at what period the ancestors of Abraham Lincoln came to America. The first account that has been obtained of them dates back about one hundred and fifty years [to around 1710], at which time they were living in Berks County, Pennsylvania, and were members of the Society of Friends [better known as Quakers, an antislavery but pacifist religion]. Whence or when they came to that region is not known.[1]

About the middle of the last century [circa 1750], the great-grandfather of Abraham Lincoln removed[2] from Berks County, Pennsylvania, to Rockingham County, Virginia. There, Abraham Lincoln, the grandfather, and Thomas Lincoln, the father of the subject of this sketch, were born.[3] Abraham, the grandfather, had four brothers—Isaac, Jacob, John, and Thomas—descendants of whom are now living in Virginia, North Carolina, Kentucky, Tennessee, and Missouri. Abraham [the grandfather] removed to Kentucky about the year 1780, and four years thereafter, while engaged in opening a farm, he was surprised and killed by Indians, leaving a widow, three sons, and two daughters.

---

[1] Scholars later learned that the paternal ancestors emigrated from England, arriving in Massachusetts in 1637. Descendants moved to Pennsylvania in the late 1600s. The mother's family is also English, but little else is certain.

[2] *Remove* could then mean *move*, i.e., to change place of residence.

[3] The grandfather was actually born in Pennsylvania; he moved to Virginia.

Ethnic Politics, 1860

In his campaign biography, Abraham Lincoln traces his ancestry to frontier Pennsylvania, and no further. Only three generations are noted. He likely knew more than he was saying. The surname "Lincoln" was prominent in New England, an area he had toured at length. Namesakes there included recent governors of Massachusetts and Maine. A family link was not hard to guess (and since confirmed).

Nevertheless, Mr. Lincoln never mentions roots in New England. His silence reflects ethnic tensions of the era. For in 1860, the greatest political divide was between white people, i.e., among the fractious British clans that colonized America centuries earlier.

So-called Yankees of New England, including Mr. Lincoln's forebears, descended from the Mayflower Pilgrims and their followers. This idealistic culture was fervently antislavery. By contrast, conservative "Cavaliers" and other ethnic groups were either indifferent or openly endorsed slavery in the Southern States.

Ethnicity and region were hence important in the politics of 1860. Mr. Lincoln was favored in Yankee-dominated regions, but also appealed to mixed areas, e.g., Pennsylvania. He ran as a moderate "Westerner," a son of today's American Midwest. He touted his own brand of conservatism, promising only to limit, not abolish slavery.

The eldest son, Mordecai, remained in Kentucky until late in life, when he removed to Hancock County, Illinois, where he shortly afterward died, and where his descendants still live. The second son, Josiah, settled many years ago on [the] Blue River in Harrison County, Indiana. The eldest daughter, Mary, was married to Ralph Crume, and some of her descendants are now living in Breckenridge County, Kentucky. The second daughter, Nancy, was married to William Brumfield, and her descendants are supposed to be living in Kentucky.

Thomas, the youngest son, and father of the subject of this sketch, by the death of his father and the very narrow circumstances of his mother, was thrown upon his own resources while yet a child. Traveling from neighborhood to neighborhood, working wherever he could find employment, he grew up literally without education. He finally settled in Hardin County [Kentucky], where in 1806 he was married to Nancy Hanks,[1] whose family had also come from Virginia [and who became the mother of Abraham Lincoln]. The fruits of this union were a daughter and two sons. One of the latter died in infancy; the daughter died later in life, having been married, but leaving no issue. The sole survivor is the subject of this sketch.

[The Missing Sister]

[Editor's Note: The coauthors Lincoln and Scripps[2] both labored on the above family history, but it is still notably lifeless. Mr. Scripps later revealed that the candidate requested that some matters be kept private. This likely included details about the "daughter" who "died later in life." She was Mr. Lincoln's sister, Sarah, born in 1807, two years before him. The siblings grew up together and suffered the death of their mother, Nancy Hanks, in an epidemic in 1818. The sister also died tragically: At age 20, she and her baby perished in childbirth. Abraham Lincoln was then only 18—the "sole survivor."

Neighbors fondly recalled the sister as the proverbial girl next door, with the same winning manner as her brother. Yet, the name of the sister, and that of a deceased infant brother, Thomas, never appear in the book. Instead, the boy Lincoln appears below as an only child. His sister, a companion of his entire childhood, is erased.

The text suggests memories of siblings had dimmed and were no longer of much import. Perhaps. Thirty years had passed. A boy became a man and ran for president. A quiet sorrow, though, perhaps lingered in other ways.]

[Birth & Childhood]

Abraham Lincoln was born in Hardin County, Kentucky, February 12, 1809 [on his father's small farm near the town of Hodgenville].[3]

[Editor's Note: The text conspicuously fails to confirm an already legendary log cabin. The omission reflects Mr. Lincoln's discomfort with myth-making; he deemed his childhood no worse than most in a frontier era. He sternly told his biographer and coauthor, John Locke Scripps, that "it is a great piece of folly to attempt to make anything out of me or my early life. It can all be condensed into a single sentence, ... 'The short and simple annals of the poor.' That's my life, and that's all you or anyone else can make out of it."

---

[1] The modern actor, Tom Hanks, may be a distant cousin of the mother.

[2] John Locke Scripps (1818-66), editor of what became the Chicago *Tribune*.

[3] This "Sinking Spring" farm is now in later-formed Larue County, Kentucky.

Symbolic Frontier Cabin
The Lincoln family perhaps had a home like this one.

[Nevertheless, Mr. Scripps privately noted that "Lincoln seemed to be painfully impressed with the extreme poverty of his early surroundings." In particular, Mr. Lincoln's youth in a slave State was primitive relative to Northern States where slavery was banned, and where modernization was under way. Below, Mr. Scripps focuses on those deprived circumstances to highlight slavery's harm to *white* people, not just to black slaves. The political symbolism is inescapable. Mr. Lincoln put aside his misgivings and consented to this informative, but unpleasant exegesis of his early years.]

It would be difficult to conceive of more unpromising circumstances than those under which he was ushered into life. His parents were poor and uneducated. They were under the social ban which the presence of slavery always entails upon poverty. Their very limited means—and the low grade of the neighboring schools —precluded the expectation of conferring upon their children the advantages of even a common English education.

The present inhabitants of the Western States [a reference to the American Midwest][1] can have but a faint idea of the schools which fifty years ago [circa 1810] constituted the only means of

---

[1]   The Free States of Ohio, Indiana, Illinois, Wisconsin, and Michigan.

education accessible to the poorer classes [in neighboring Kentucky, a slave State]. The teachers were, for the most part, ignorant, uncultivated men—rough of speech, uncouth in manners, and rarely competent to teach beyond the simplest rudiments of learning: "spelling, reading, writing," and sometimes a very little arithmetic. The books of study then in vogue would not now be tolerated in schools of the lowest grade. The schoolhouse—constructed of logs [and being] floorless, windowless, and without enclosure [having only one room]—was in admirable harmony with teacher, text-books, and the mode of imparting instruction.

In his seventh year, Abraham was sent for short periods to two of these schools, and while attending them, progressed so far as to learn to write. For this acquirement, he manifested a great fondness.

Abraham Lincoln
his hand and pen .
he will be good but
god knows When

Early Writing, Age 14

Herndon, 1895

It was his custom to form letters, to write words and sentences wherever he found suitable material. He scrawled them with charcoal; he scored them in the dust, in the sand, in the snow—anywhere and everywhere that lines could be drawn, there he improved his capacity for writing.

Meanwhile, the worldly condition of the elder Lincoln [Abraham's father] did not improve. He realized in his daily experience and observation how slavery oppresses the poorer classes, making their poverty and social disrepute a permanent condition through the degradation which it affixes to labor. Revolving this matter in his mind, he wisely resolved to remove his young family from its presence.

Accordingly, in the autumn of 1816, he emigrated to Spencer County, Indiana—one of the States consecrated forever to freedom and free labor by the Jeffersonian Ordinance of 1787. [The latter was the Northwest Ordinance of Thomas Jefferson, forever banning slavery in the then frontier lands of the American Midwest] and which, with the States now comprising the territory included in that memorable instrument, has afforded asylum—an open field and fair play—to thousands upon thousands who have, in like manner, been driven from their homes by [competition with slavery]—that great social scourge of the "poor whites" of the South.

Young Lincoln was in his eighth year when the family removed to Indiana. They settled in an unbroken forest, gladly taking upon themselves all the privations and hardships of a pioneer life; [they felt fortunate] in view of what they had left behind them.

The erection of a house and the felling of the forest was the first work to be done. Abraham was young to engage in such labor, but he was large of his age, stalwart, and willing to work. An ax was at once placed in his hands, and from that time until he attained his twenty-third year, when not employed in labor on the farm, he was almost constantly wielding that most useful implement.

Traditional Farming[1]

Upon the arrival of the family in Indiana, the friends who were left behind [in Kentucky] were to be written to. The elder Lincoln could do nothing more in the way of writing than to bunglingly sign his name.[2] The mother, though a ready reader, had not been taught the accomplishment of writing.[3]

In this emergency, Abraham's skill as a penman was put into requisition, and with highly satisfactory results. From that time onward, he conducted the family correspondence. This fact soon be-

---

[1] Scene is Oklahoma in 1917, a century after Mr. Lincoln's childhood.

[2] "Bunglingly" is Mr. Lincoln's harsh word for his father's illiteracy.

[3] Some modern historians are uncertain about her reading skills.

coming public, little Abraham was considered a marvel of learning and wisdom by the simple-minded settlers; and ever afterward, as long as he remained in Indiana, he was the letter writer for the neighbors generally, as well as for his father's family.

That he was selected for this purpose was doubtless owing not more to his proficiency in writing than to his ability to express the wishes and feelings of those for whom he wrote in clear and forcible language, and to that obliging disposition that has always distinguished him in subsequent life. It cannot be doubted that something of Mr. Lincoln's style and facility of composition in later years, both as a writer and speaker, is to be traced back to these earlier efforts as an amanuensis[1] for the neighborhood.

In the autumn of 1818, Abraham, in the loss of his mother, experienced the first great sorrow of his life. Facts in the possession of the writer have impressed him with the belief that, although of but limited education, she was a woman of great native strength of intellect and force of character; and he suspects that those admirable qualities of head and heart which characterize her distinguished son are inherited mostly from her.

[Editor's Note: John Locke Scripps wrote the above passage, but his "facts" come from Abraham Lincoln. The latter favored his mother—and was biased against his father, Thomas Lincoln, e.g., "bunglingly."

The bias was so strong, that the son refused to visit his father on his deathbed. Neither Lincoln ever explained the bias. The father was kindly, hardworking, more successful than many, and passed on priceless hereditary attributes. The family tree in both England and America included many politicians, a fact Abraham Lincoln may have discovered by 1860.

Nevertheless, father and son took their dispute and its undisclosed origin to their graves. However, the son's biography awkwardly avoids this topic as well as his sister's early death. Were the matters related? Young Abraham Lincoln bore open grudges against his in-laws, possibly for mistreatment of his sister. Did he also blame his father for not intervening on her behalf?]

[Parents' Religion]

She [Lincoln's mother], as well as her husband, was a devout member of the Baptist Church. It was her custom on the Sabbath, when there was no religious worship in the neighborhood—a thing

---

[1] An *amanuensis* takes dictation from important people.

Thomas Lincoln (1778-1851)
Father

He and his son Abraham were on difficult terms. This unverified portrait may date to 1850.

Library of Congress

of frequent occurrence—to employ a portion of the day in reading the Scriptures aloud to her family.[1] After Abraham and his sister had learned to read, they shared by turns in this duty of Sunday reading.

This practice, continued faithfully through a series of years, could not fail to produce certain effects. Among other things, its tendency was to impart an accurate acquaintance with Bible history and Bible teachings; and it must also have been largely instrumental in developing the religious element in the character of the younger members of the family.

The facts correspond with this hypothesis. There are few men in public life so familiar with the Scriptures as Mr. Lincoln. [To the Bible, he owes the religious metaphors of his speeches], while to those pious labors of his mother in his early childhood, are doubtless to be attributed much of that purity of life, that elevation of moral character, that exquisite sense of justice, and that sentiment of humanity which now form distinguishing traits of his character.

A year after the death of his mother, his father married Mrs. Sally Johnston at Elizabethtown, Kentucky. A widow with three

---

[1] Like her son, she may have recited Scriptures from memory.

Sarah Bush Lincoln (1789-1869)
Stepmother

Abraham Lincoln adored her. In 1865, she mourned the loss of her "boy." Her expression tells all.

Tarbell, 1896

children, she proved a good and kind mother to Abraham.[1] She survives her husband, and is now living in Coles County, Illinois.

[Editor's Note: After a long illness, Abraham's father, Thomas Lincoln, died at age 73 on January 17, 1851, near Farmington, Illinois. Historians usually identify his second wife, Abraham's stepmother, as *Sarah* Bush Johnston. Her stepson, though, knew her as "Sally," a nickname. It is one of many telltale words and phrases that point to Abraham Lincoln's coauthorship. His biographer, Mr. Scripps, only halfheartedly disguises his subject's role.]

After the removal of the family to Indiana, Abraham attended school a little, chiefly in the winter, when work was less pressing; but the aggregate of all the time thus spent, both in Kentucky and Indiana, did not amount to one year. He is therefore indebted to schools for but a very small part of his education.

[Self-Made Man]

All men who become in any respect distinguished, are, in one sense at least, self-made. That is to say, the development and the discipline of the intellect can only be secured by self-effort. Without this, assistance on the part of teachers, however long and continuously offered, will yield no fruit. With it, assistance is valuable mainly in that it directs and encourages effort.

---

[1] The 1860 text is "kind mother *to to* Abraham," a typographical error.

[However, consider another definition of "self-made":] He is said to be a self-made man who attains to distinction [or success in life] without having enjoyed the advantages of teachers and of institutions of learning. And in this sense, Abraham Lincoln is peculiarly entitled to the appellation. His early teachers were men of scarcely any learning, and what he mastered through their assistance, consisted only of the simplest rudiments of education.

That subsequent training and disciplining of the intellect, that habit of close investigation, that power of intense thought, which enable him to master every subject he investigates, and that faculty of clear and forcible expression, of logical arrangement, and of overwhelming argument, by which he enforces his own well-grounded convictions—all this is the result of his own unaided exertions, and of a naturally sound and vigorous understanding.

So, far from being indebted to institutions of learning for any of the qualities which characterize him, he [Lincoln] was never in a college or an academy as a student, and was never in fact inside of a college or academy building until after he had commenced the practice of the law. He studied English grammar after he was twenty-three years of age. At twenty-five, he mastered enough of geometry, trigonometry, and mensuration to enable him to take the field as a surveyor. And he studied the six books of Euclid [a classical treatise on geometry and mathematics] after he had served a term in Congress, and when he was forty years of age, amid the pressure of an extensive legal practice, and of frequent demands upon his time by the public.

Books were another means of education which young Lincoln did not neglect; but, in a backwoods settlement of Indiana forty years ago [circa 1820], books were somewhat rarer than now. They [the books] had this advantage, however, over a majority of the books of the present time: The few that were to be had, possessed solid merit and well repaid the time and labor given to their study. Abraham's first book, after *Dilworth's Spelling-Book*, was, as has been stated, the Bible. Next to that came *Æsop's Fables*, which he read with great zest, and so often as to commit the whole to memory. After that, he obtained a copy of *Pilgrim's Progress*—a book which perhaps has quickened as many dormant intellects, and started into vigorous growth the religious element of as many natures, as any other in the English language.[1]

Then came the *Life of Franklin*, Weems's *Washington*, and Riley's *Narrative* [all bestselling biographies].[2] Over the two former [*Franklin* and *Washington*], the boy lingered with rapt delight. He followed [George] Washington and brave Ben Franklin through their early trials and struggles, as well as through their later triumphs; and even then, in the midst of his cramped surroundings, and in the face of the discouragements which beset him on every hand, his soul was lifted upwards. And noble aspirations, which never afterwards forsook him, grew up within him, and great thoughts stirred his bosom—thoughts of emancipated nations, of the glorious principles which lie at the foundation of human freedom, and of honorable fame acquired by heroic endeavors to enforce and maintain them. These books constituted the boy's library.

[Will Work for a Book]

When he [Abraham] was fourteen or fifteen years of age, he learned that one Mr. Crawford, a distant neighbor, had in his house Ramsey's *[sic] Life of Washington*—a book which he was told gave a fuller and better account of Washington and the Revolution than the volume he had read with so much pleasure. He at once borrowed the book and devoured its contents.[3]

---

[1] *Pilgrim's Progress* by John Bunyan is a spiritual allegory of humanity's common journey through life. First published in 1678, it remains popular today.

[2] Life stories of Benjamin Franklin and George Washington, plus James Riley's *Authentic Narrative,* an 1817 memoir of castaways enslaved in Morocco.

[3] Mr. Scripps may have confused David Ramsay's *The Life of George Washington,* published in 1811; and the revised 1806 edition, or later, of Mason L. Weems's *Life of Washington*. The latter first related the boy Washington chopping down a cherry tree. In 1861, President-elect Lincoln told an audience in New Jersey that "in my childhood—the earliest days of my being able to read— I got hold of a small book, such a one as few of the younger members have ever seen—Weems's *Life of Washington*. I remember all the accounts there given of the battlefields and struggles for the liberties of the country."

Lincoln's Washington

Poverty and frontier isolation engulfed Abraham Lincoln as a child. However, there was a bright spot—a handful of books borrowed from his kindly stepmother and generous neighbors.

A lasting imprint resulted. For example, the New Testament of the Bible reverberated decades later in his "House Divided" speech, a poignant warning of conflict over slavery.

However, less known is the Life of Washington *by Mason L. Weems. This mythic tale exalted George Washington's virtue, inspiring the boy Lincoln to emulate an iconic hero. In their youth, both men rafted down western rivers; surveyed frontier lands; led militia against Indians; and served in new state legislatures.*

George Washington
First U.S. President

Alas, young Mr. Lincoln never found the glory that was George Washington. An icon and his era could not be repeated. However, the adult Mr. Lincoln embarked on his own unique quest for virtue. Surprisingly, his life as a frontier lawyer and antislavery firebrand led right back to dreams of childhood. Mr. Lincoln became a great president and wartime leader, just like George Washington. Their common quest for virtue—to do the right thing—still inspires people of goodwill everywhere.

[However] by some accident, the volume was exposed to a shower [during a rainstorm] and badly damaged. Young Lincoln had no money, but he knew how to work. He went to Crawford, told him what had happened, and expressed his readiness to work out the full value of the book. Crawford had a field of corn which had been stripped of the blades as high as the ear, preparatory to cutting off the tops for winter fodder for his cattle. He expressed his willingness to square accounts if Lincoln would cut the tops from that field of corn. The offer was promptly accepted; and with three days of hard labor, the book was paid for; and young Lincoln returned home the proud possessor of another volume.

Not long after this incident, he was fortunate enough to get possession of a copy of Plutarch's *Lives* [a heroic biography of ancient statesmen]. What fields of thought its perusal opened up to the stripling,[1] what hopes were excited in his youthful breast, what worthy models of probity, of justice, of honor, and of devotion to great principles he resolved to pattern after, can be readily imagined by those who are familiar with his subsequent career, and who have themselves lingered over the same charmed page[s].

[Editor's Note: Writing in haste, the biographer Mr. Scripps erred in the above passage: The boy Lincoln never read Plutarch's *Lives*. Noticing the mistake only after publication, a nervous Mr. Scripps urged the candidate to quickly read Plutarch. Mr. Lincoln, renown for devotion to truth, dutifully complied, albeit with a seriousness that was distinctly tongue-in-cheek.[2]]

[Preachers & Sermons]

Listening occasionally to the early backwoods preachers was another means which, more than schools, and perhaps quite as much as books, aided in developing and forming the character of young Lincoln. It has already been stated that his parents were pious members of the Baptist Church, [but] among the backwoodsmen of Indiana at that period, sectarianism did not run as high as it probably does in the same section now [in 1860]. The people were glad of an opportunity to hear a sermon, whether delivered by one of their own religious faith or not.

Thus it was [that many denomination were heard], at least with the father and mother of young Lincoln. [They were devout parents] who never failed to attend with their family upon religious worship, whenever held within reasonable distance. They gladly received the Word, caring less for the doctrinal tenets of the preacher, than for the earnestness and zeal with which he enforced practical godliness.

---

[1]   *Stripling* is an antiquated word for a fledging young man.

[2]   Ida Tarbell, *The Life of Abraham Lincoln*, 4 vol. (New York: Lincoln History Society, 1907), I: 29n-30n.

Itinerant Preacher
Rural Kentucky, 1940

*For centuries, traveling ministers spread
the Gospel to frontier America. They introduced the boy Lincoln to religious oratory, subtly shaping his future.*

Library of Congress

   [Regarding itinerant preachers] no class of men are more de-
serving of admiration than those who have been the first to carry
the Gospel to our frontier settlements. If ever men have labored in
the cause of their Divine Master, and for the salvation of their fellow mortals, impelled by motives entirely free from any dross of
selfishness, surely that honor should be awarded to them.

   Many of these early pioneer preachers were gifted with a rare
eloquence. Inspired always with the grandeur of their theme, com-
muning daily with nature while on their long and solitary journey-
ings from settlement to settlement, they seemed to be favored, beyond human wont [or ability], with a very near approach to the
source of all inspiration; and coming with this preparation before
an audience of simple-minded settlers—preacher and people freed
from conventional restraint—these men almost always moved the
hearts and wrought upon the imagination of their hearers as only
those gifted with the truest eloquence can.

   Of course, the immediate result of such preaching was to awak-
en the religious element, rather than to inform the understanding

Spiritual Lincoln

Mr. Lincoln's biography honestly praises his embrace of Christianity. However, the book omits a sensitive fact: He never formally joined a church. In his opinion, no sect was entirely true to Jesus Christ.

This skepticism of churches began when Mr. Lincoln was a young man. He witnessed affluent churchgoers disdain the poor and tolerate slavery. He stayed apart and studied the Bible on his own.

Nevertheless, some opponents castigated Mr. Lincoln as hostile to religion. Alas, during his presidential campaign, he could say little in his own defense; discretion was the better part of valor.

For in 1860, religion was in turmoil. The dispute over slavery had deeply divided the Protestant churches. Atoning for past failings, congregations of the Northern States now condemned slavery. Many of the slave South retorted that the Bible endorsed slavery. Several denominations angrily split apart, North and South.

As a compromise, Abraham Lincoln and his family quietly attended the Presbyterian Church in his wife's name. Ultimately, though, he developed his own theology. Hallowing justice for all, a nation under God, and "a new birth of Freedom," President Lincoln became the greatest spiritual leader ever to occupy the White House.

Library of Congress

Lincoln Family Pew

as to doctrines and dogmas—to lead to spiritual exaltation and religious fervor, rather than to a clear knowledge and appreciation of
those points of theological controversy which, for so many centuries, have engaged the attention of disputatious divines.

It is not intended to decide which of the two methods [inspired
preaching, or a theological discourse] is the better calculated to
evangelize the world. But as to the great value of the preaching
here spoken of, and its singular adaptation to the people to whom
it was addressed, there can be but one opinion: That it exerted a
marked influence upon the character of young Lincoln, that it thoroughly awakened the religious element within him, and that his
subsequent life has been greatly influenced by it. [These] are facts
which the writer desires to place upon record for the encourage-
ment of other laborers in the same field, and as a distinct recognition of the further fact that there can be no true and lasting greatness unless its foundation be laid in the truths of the Bible.

[Frontier Laborer]

And thus young Lincoln grew to manhood, constantly engaged
in the various kinds of labor incident to the country and the times
—felling the forest, clearing the ground of the undergrowth and of
logs; splitting rails; pulling the crosscut and the whipsaw; driving
the frower;[1] plowing, harrowing, planting, hoeing, harvesting;
[and] assisting at house-raisings, logrollings, and cornhuskings. [He
was] mingling cordially with the simpleminded honest people with
whom his lot was cast, developing a kindly nature, and evincing
social qualities which rendered his companionship desirable. Remarkable even then for a wonderful gift of relating anecdotes, and
for a talent of interspersing them with acute and apt reflections,
[he was] everywhere a favorite, always simple, genial, truthful, and
unpretending; and always chosen umpire on occasions calling for
the exercise of sound judgment and inflexible impartiality.

It is scarcely necessary to add that he also greatly excelled in
all those homely feats of strength, agility, and endurance practiced

---

[1] A *frower* is a mechanical device for splitting wood into staves or shingles.

by frontier people in his sphere of life. In wrestling, jumping, running, throwing the maul, and pitching the crowbar,[1] he always stood first among those of his own age. As in height, he loomed above all his associates, so in these customary pastimes, he far surpassed his youthful competitors;[2] and even when pitted against those of maturer years, he was almost always victorious.

J.G. Ferris, 1909/Library of Congress

Working Man
Artist's depiction of Abraham Lincoln making fences.

In such daily companionship, he grew up in full sympathy with the people, rejoicing in their simple joys and pleasures, sorrowing in their trials and misfortunes, and united to them all by that bond of brotherhood among the honest poor—a common heritage of labor.

---

[1] A *maul* is a heavy sledgehammer. It and the crowbar are tests of strength.

[2] The 1860 text is "he *as* far surpassed," a probable error.

Chapter Two
Removal to Illinois

Illinois in 1829—Explorers in the Northern and Middle Portion of the State
—Character of the Country—Remarkable Influx of Population—Removal of
the Lincoln Family—Their Mode of Travel—Founding Another Home—
Building a Log Cabin and Making Rails—Symbols.

Fran 1829 until the financial revulsion of 1837-40 [a deep
economic recession], a vast flood of immigration poured into
Illinois [from the Eastern United States]. [In 1840, the population of Illinois reached 476,000, a threefold increase.]

At the first-named date [1829], the population of the State was
only about 150,000—a number scarcely equal to the present population of the city of Chicago [in 1860]. This population was confined mostly to the southern part of the State. There were comparatively few people north of Alton [a town on the Mississippi River,
about twenty miles north of St. Louis], and these, as is always the
case in the settlement of a new country, were scattered along the
rivers and smaller watercourses. And even south of Alton, in the
older-settled portion of the State, most of the population still clung
either to the watercourses or close to the edges of the timberland.[1]

The large prairies, with the exception of a narrow belt along the
fringes of timber [lining the rivers], were wholly uncultivated and
without population. Indeed, at that time, and for many years after,
it was the opinion of even the most intelligent people, that the larger prairies of Illinois would never be used for any other purpose
than as a common pasturage for the cattle of adjacent settlers. It is
only of later years, and since the introduction of railroads, that the
true value and destiny of these prairies have come to be understood and appreciated. [The prairies became vast farmlands after
railroads provided a quick means for crops to reach market.]

Thus, in 1829, only an infinitesimal portion of the better part
of Illinois was occupied. At the same time, the people of the other

---

[1] This passage subtly foreshadows dramatic events in Alton. See page 171.

Americans Go West

Abraham Lincoln's biography romanticized the trek of everyday fam-
ilies into the American West. Slave owners, though, staked their own
claim to these vast new lands, setting the stage for conflict.

States entertained very imperfect notions of the character of the country and of its wonderful natural resources. The first settlement by an indigenous American population had been the result of the accounts carried back to the old States [the original thirteen colonies] by the soldiers who accompanied the gallant George Rogers Clark in that memorable expedition in 1778, which resulted in the conquest of Kaskaskia [and] Cahokia [Illinois], and Vincennes [Indiana]. Another impetus was given in the same direction after the war of 1812, by similar reports of the beauty and fertility of the country taken back by rangers and other troops who had done service in the then Territory of Illinois.[1]

But from that time until the year 1829, the increase of population [in Illinois] by immigration had been very slow. The era of financial prosperity which terminated in the memorable financial breakdown of 1837-40, gave another impulse to Western immigration [from the older States of the East]. The Anglo-Saxon greed for

---

[1] *Territory* refers to areas with too few people for statehood, and no votes in federal elections. Residents, though, can vote for local territorial legislatures.

land was stimulated to unusual activity by the abundance of money [from the economic boom of the early 1830s], and explorers started out in search of new and desirable countries.

Entering Illinois by the great lines of travel—at Vincennes, at Terre Haute [Indiana]; at Paducah [Kentucky]; at Shawneetown [Illinois]—and journeying westward and northward, these explorers were struck with the wonderful beauty and fertility of the country, and the ease with which it could be reduced to immediate cultivation. Its rich, undulating prairies; its vast natural pasturage for cattle; the accessibility to navigable watercourses; the salubrity of its climate; and above all, its millions of acres of government land [for distribution to settlers], conspired to render it peculiarly attractive to men who had been accustomed all their lives to mountainous and rocky districts, or to a country covered with heavy forests.

Other explorers, entering the State [Illinois] from the direction of the great Northwestern Lakes [now called the Great Lakes], and traversing it southward and westward to the Mississippi [River], saw, at every stage of their journey, a country no less fertile and inviting—the sylvan beauty of which no pen or pencil could adequately portray. The reports spread by these travelers on their return to the older States, regarding the wonderful region they had seen—together with occasional letters contributed to leading journals by delighted and enthusiastic tourists—awakened a spirit of emigration the like of which the country had never before witnessed. The stream of population that set at once Illinois-ward continued, from this and other causes, to grow constantly broader and deeper.

[People were] coming in from the South, setting westward from the belt of Middle States, [and] pouring in by way of the Northwestern Lakes. [The emigrants were] dotting every prairie with new homes; opening thousands of farms; making roads; building bridges; founding schools, churches, villages, and cities—until the Crash of 1837 [a severe economic recession] came suddenly and unexpectedly upon the country, putting an immediate and effectual check upon the human movement.

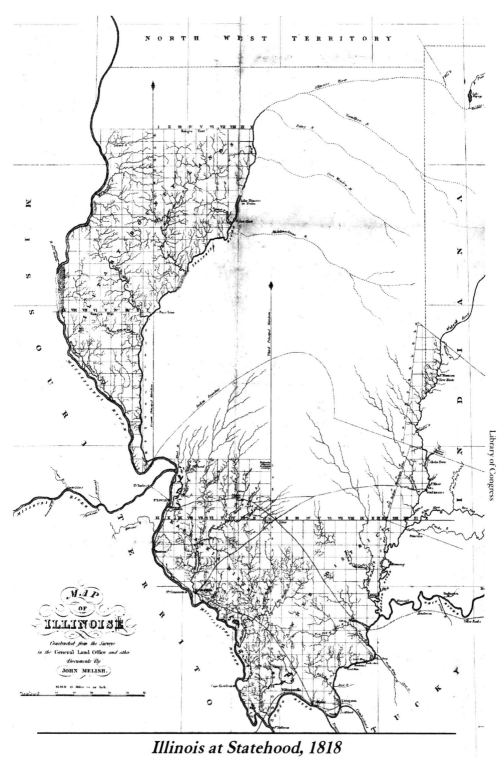

Illinois at Statehood, 1818

Springfield and Chicago are literally not yet on the map (upper right).

Among those who heard the earliest reports concerning this land of promise, were the Lincoln family in their quiet home in Indiana, and they resolved to try their fortunes in it. Accordingly, on the first day of March 1830, Abraham, having just completed his twenty-first year, [and] his father and family,[1] together with the families of the two daughters and sons-in-law of his stepmother, bidding *adieu* to the old homestead in Indiana, turned their faces towards Illinois.

[Ox-Drawn Wagons]

In those days, when people changed their residence from one State or settlement to another, they took all their movable possessions with them—their household goods, their kitchen utensils (including provisions for the journey), their farming implements—[and] their horses and cattle. The former [their possessions] were loaded into wagons drawn, for the most part, by oxen; and the latter [their livestock] were driven by the smaller boys of the family, who were sometimes assisted by their sisters and mother.

Thus arranged for a journey of weeks—not unfrequently of months—the emigrant set out, thinking but little of the hardships before him—of bad roads, of unbridged streams, of disagreeable weather, of sleeping on the ground or in the wagon, of sickness, accidents, and, sometimes, death by the way. [Rather, he was] dwelling chiefly in thought upon the novelty and excitement of the trip, the rumored attractions of the new country whither he was going, and of the probable advantages likely to result from the change.

By stages of ten or fifteen miles per day over untraveled roads—now across mountains, swamps, and watercourses; and now through dense umbrageous forests; and across broad prairies where the horizon alone bounded the vision—the caravan of wagons, men, women and children, flocks and herds, toiled onward by day, sleeping under the broad canopy of stars by night, [and] patiently accomplishing the destined journey, sometimes of weeks', sometimes of months' duration.

---

[1] *Family* here refers to his stepmother and her children. Abraham's older sister, Sarah, died in childbirth in 1828, two years earlier.

Library of Congress

Covered Wagons Pulled by Oxen
As late as the 1890s, ox-drawn wagons like those of Mr. Lincoln's youth were still in service. Note the small boy prodding oxen (right rear).

It was by this primitive and laborious method that the Lincoln family made the journey [in 1830] from Spencer County, Indiana, to Macon County, Illinois—Abraham himself driving one of the ox-teams. He had now arrived at manhood [age 21], and both by law and by universal custom, was at liberty to begin the world for himself. But he was the only son of his father, now advanced in years, and it was not in his nature to desert his aged sire at a time when all the hardships, privations, and toil of making a new home in a new country, were about to be entered upon. Whatever the future may have seemed to hold in it as a reward for effort specially directed to that end, he cheerfully put aside in obedience to his sense of duty, and engaged at once and heartily in the work before him.

That summer's labor consisted mainly in building a log house, into which the family moved; making rails for, and fencing in ten acres of prairie; [and] breaking the sod, and raising upon it a crop of corn. This farm was situated on the north side of the Sangamon River, at the junction of the timber land and prairie, and about ten miles west of Decatur [Illinois].

Abraham Lincoln and Economic Progress

Abraham Lincoln never forgot his humble roots as the child of struggling farmers. Throughout his political career, he promised an activist government that would aid everyday people—the American future would be free, not slave. Upon becoming president, he quickly honored that promise. His early policies included:

- *a ban on slavery in the new Territories of the American West;*
- *a homestead program to give land to family farmers;*
- *new public colleges for the States ("land-grant" colleges);*
- *protection of high-wage jobs and industries by imposing a high tariff, or tax, on foreign-made products; and*
- *initiating major transportation projects, e.g., the first transcontinental railroad linking the East and West Coasts.*

Mr. Lincoln's High Technology

In the aftermath of victory in the American Civil War, a series of U.S. presidents expanded upon the above policies. Freedom, not slavery, prevailed in the United States. The prosperous American middle-class of the following century was Abraham Lincoln's ultimate legacy.

[To assist his father, young Mr. Lincoln used an ax to cut down trees and split them into fence rails.] The rails used in fencing-in the ten-acre field are those of which so much of late has been said in the newspapers [in the spring and summer of 1860]. [Regarding the rails] their existence was brought to the public attention during the sitting of the Republican State Convention at Decatur, on the ninth of May last, on which occasion, a banner attached to two of these rails, and bearing an appropriate inscription, was brought into the assemblage and formally presented to that body [by John Hanks, a Lincoln cousin], amid a scene of unparalleled enthusiasm.

Since then, they [the fence rails made by Mr. Lincoln] have been in great demand [as symbols of freedom] in every State of the Union[1] in which free labor [rather than slave labor] is honored— where they have been borne in processions of the people; and hailed by hundreds of thousands of freemen as a symbol of triumph; and as a glorious vindication of freedom, and of the rights and the dignity of free labor.[2]

These, however, were far from being the first or only rails made by young Lincoln. He was a practiced hand at the business. His first lessons had been taken while yet a boy in Indiana. Some of the rails made by him in that State have been clearly identified, and are now eagerly sought after. The writer has seen a cane, now in the possession of Mr. Lincoln, made since his nomination by one of his old Indiana acquaintances from one of those rails split by his own hands in boyhood.

[Editor's Note: Mr. Lincoln's biography emphasizes his farming and working-class origins, because in 1860 most voters worked on farms or in primitive factories. Conditions were often grueling and dangerous. Through personal experience, Mr. Lincoln knows the workers' lot and will be *their* president.]

---

[1] *Union* is shorthand for the United States of America and refers to the federal system binding the States in a single country. *Union* has patriotic connotations, celebrating national existence. America won that existence only after a long War of Independence, 1775-83, which in 1860 was scarcely a lifetime past.

[2] *Free labor* refers to *paid* workers with personal freedom and constitutional rights, i.e., they are not slaves.

Chapter Three
Flatboatman—Clerk—Indian-Fighter

Flatboats and Flatboatmen—A Commercial Revolution—The Deep Snow—
Lincoln Engages to Take a Flatboat to New Orleans—Incident of His First
Trip—First Entrance into Sangamon County—Builds a Boat and Goes to
New Orleans—Takes Charge of a Store and Mill at New Salem—Primitive
Customs—Personal Popularity—The Black Hawk War—Volunteers—Elect-
ed Captain—Volunteers a Second and Third Time—The War Ended—Re-
turn Home.

[Editor's Note: The Midwestern frontier of Mr. Lincoln's youth was
primitive. Manufactured goods, e.g., textiles and tools, were not made locally,
but were bought from the East Coast. To earn cash for these purchases, frontier residents shipped farm products on large rafts, or "flatboats," down wild
rivers to distant settlements. A favorite destination was New Orleans, a
bustling port flush with wealth from sugar, cotton—and slavery. At age 19, a
penniless (and naive) Mr. Lincoln took a job on a flatboat and made the long
journey into the Southern States. His book introduces the tale with an economic history of the early Midwest. Colorful adventures soon unfold.]

Those who have come into Illinois since steamboats became
numerous on the Western waters [the rivers and lakes of
the American Midwest], and since the introduction of railroads, and the opening of the Illinois and Michigan Canal [in
1848], have no correct idea how small an amount of business was
transacted in the State so late as 1830 [only thirty years before the
presidential election of 1860], or of the great commercial revolution which has taken place since that time.

At the period named, there was but little inducement for growing surplus productions. [Farmers grew crops only for home con-
sumption, not for cash sales.] The merchants of the country [who
sold "dry goods," e.g., clothing and hardware][1] did not deal in
corn, wheat, flour, beef, pork, lard, butter, or any of the great sta-
ples of the State. Beyond the purchase of a few furs and peltries,[2]

---

[1]   Merchants, or "general stores," in the Midwest were forerunners of famous
department stores, including Sears and Marshall Fields in Chicago, Illinois.

[2]   *Peltries* refers to pelts, or animal skins used for leather.

D.W.C. Peters, 1880

Flatboat

Flatboats derived their name from their shape. Animals were often among the passengers. Young Mr. Lincoln ferried hogs.

[or] small quantities of feathers, beeswax, and tallow, the merchant rarely engaged in barter [or trading farm products].

The old United States Bank [backed by the federal government] was then in existence, and through it, the exchanges of the country were conducted at a rate so satisfactory that no Western[1] merchant thought of shipping the products of the country to liquidate his Eastern balances. [The local merchant borrowed from the Bank, rather than sell farm products to repay suppliers back East.] He bought his goods for cash (or on credit) and collected his debts [from local customers, mostly poor farmers], if so fortunate as to collect at all, in the same commodity, and never paid any of it out again, except for goods [i.e., more inventory to sell].

[Hence, the frontier country always needed more cash to send to the East for manufactured goods.] The dependence of the country for money was chiefly upon that brought in by new settlers. Occasionally an adventurer appeared who paid out money for sufficient of the products [from farmers] of the country to load a flatboat, which he floated off to find a market [and recoup his investment]. Sometimes the more enterprising of the farmers, finding no market at home for the surplus of their farms, loaded a flatboat on

---

[1] *Western* could then refer to any area west of the original thirteen colonies. *Eastern* refers to those former colonies, i.e., States of the East Coast.

their own account [and shipped it to a distant market], and by this means some money found its way into the country.

Within the last twenty years [1840-60] this order of things has entirely changed, and at the present time, every description of surplus product meets a ready cash market at home [in the new cities of the Midwest, e.g., Chicago]. While the old order lasted, however, the business of shipping by flatboats was maintained on all the Western rivers, though the multiplication and competition of steamboats rendered the number less every year.

The business itself [manning crop-laden flatboats], was one of exposure [to extreme weather], of hard labor, and of constant peril. It developed and nurtured a race of men peculiar for courage, herculean strength, hardihood, and great contempt of danger. Western annals abound in stories of these men. As a class they have become extinct, and the world will never see their like again; but their memory remains and will constitute a part of the country's history, and mingle with our national romance forever.

[Thus concludes a summary of early Midwestern history.] This much it seemed necessary to say for the benefit of the uninitiated reader, by way of preface to some account of young Lincoln's experiences as a flatboatman. Going back then to the new home on the Sangamon River, we take up again the thread of the narrative:

[Winter of 1830-31]

The winter of 1830-31 is memorable to this day among the early settlers of Illinois, by reason of the deep snow which fell about the last of December, and which continued upon the ground for more than two months. It was a season of unusual severity, both upon the settlers and their [live]stock. Many of the latter perished from exposure to the cold and from hunger, while the former [the settlers], especially the more recently arrived of their number, were often put to great straits to obtain provisions. Of these hardships, the Lincolns and their immediate neighbors had their full share, and but for Abraham, whose vigor of constitution and remarkable power of endurance fitted him for long and wearisome journeys in search of provisions, their suffering would have been often greater.

[To further help his family, Mr. Lincoln found a job on a flat-boat.] Some time during the winter, one of those adventurers previously spoken of, Denton Offutt, engaged in buying a boatload of produce to ship in the spring [and] fell in with young Lincoln [hiring him as a crewman]. Conceiving a liking for him, and having learned also that he had previously taken a flatboat down the Mississippi [River], Offutt engaged him, together with his stepmother's son, John D. Johnston, and his mother's cousin, John Hanks, to take a flatboat from Beardstown on the Illinois River to New Orleans [a 700-mile journey into slaveholding States of the South].

[Previous Flatboat Trip]

[Before discussing further the above expedition of 1831, a previous trip on a flatboat is worth noting.] Lincoln's first trip to New Orleans had been made [three years earlier, in March 1828] from the Ohio River, while living in Indiana, and when he was in the nineteenth year of his age. On that occasion also, he was a hired hand merely, and he and the son of the owner, without other assistance, made the trip [down the length of the Mississippi River].

A part of the cargo [of their flatboat] had been selected with special reference to the wants of the sugar plantations [in Southern States],[1] and the young adventurers were instructed to linger upon the sugar coast[2] for the purpose of disposing of it. On one occasion, they tied up their boat for the night near a plantation [near Baton Rouge] at which they had been trading during the afternoon.

The Negroes [local slaves] observing that the boat was in [the] charge of but two persons [Lincoln and his crewmate], seven of them formed a plan to rob it during the night. Their intention evidently was to murder the young men, rob the boat of whatever money there might be on it, carry off such articles as they could secrete in their cabins, and then by sinking the boat, destroy all traces of their guilt. They had not, however, properly estimated the courage and prowess of the two young men in charge. The latter,

---

[1]   The cargo probably included corn and small livestock, e.g., hogs.

[2]   Areas where sugarcane was grown upon plantations worked by slaves.

being on their guard, gave the would-be robbers and assassins a warm reception (and notwithstanding the disparity in numbers).

After a severe struggle in which both Lincoln and his companion were considerably hurt, the former [the slaves] were driven from the boat. At the close of the fight, the young navigators lost no time in getting their boat again under way. [Yet] the trip, in the main, was successful, and in due time, the young men returned to their homes in Indiana [after delivering cargo to New Orleans].

[Editor's Note: The above story of 1828 comes directly from Mr. Lincoln and is politically odd. Some of his opponents engaged in racist smears, claiming he would unleash black slaves to threaten white people. Mr. Lincoln defended himself and the slaves, but his hair-raising story of an assault seems to undercut him. The story also raises the question whether Mr. Lincoln was appealing to "law and order," i.e., illustrating his toughness on criminals of any color. Adding to the confusion, his aides later hinted that he blamed not the black slaves, but a white master who may have ordered the assault.

However, a simpler explanation exists: Mr. Lincoln was a well-known devotee of folklore. He unabashedly took pride in a life-and-death tale about himself as a teenager. Mr. Lincoln embarked on this first river journey to New Orleans only weeks after the heartbreaking loss of his sister on January 20, 1828. (See page 29.) As in ages past, a young man's long voyage—and trial by combat—was cathartic, a welcome release from the bitterness of life's sorrows. Few doubted his tale, and opponents little mentioned it.]

[Second Trip]

[Three years passed. Mr. Lincoln moved with his family from Indiana to Illinois. As noted above, in early 1831, a businessman, Denton Offutt, hired him to take another flatboat to New Orleans.] Lincoln and his associates [planned to float down the Mississippi River] for a second trip. Johnston and Hanks [his stepbrother and cousin respectively][1] were to join Offutt[2] at Springfield, Illinois, as soon as the snow had disappeared, whence they were to go with him to Beardstown, the port of departure for New Orleans.

[However] when the snow melted, which was about the first of March, the whole country was so flooded as to render traveling impracticable. This led the party to purchase a canoe, in which they

---

[1]   John D. Johnston and John Hanks; spelled here as *Johnson* in the 1860 text.

[2]   Spelled here as *Offut* in the 1860 text.

Frontier River

Abraham Lincoln's adventures may have influenced the young Mark Twain and his Huckleberry Finn, *also a tale of slavery and rafting down the Mississippi. Image is an 1847 print of George C. Bingham's "The Jolly Flatboat Men."*

descended the Sangamon River to a point within a few miles of Springfield [the future state capital of Illinois].

This was the time [March 1831], and this the method, of Lincoln's first entrance into Sangamon County—a county which was to be the field of his future triumphs [as a politician and lawyer]; [and] which was to become proud of him as her most distinguished citizen; and which, in time, was to be honored through him with being the home of a president of the United States.[1]

On arriving at Springfield, they learned from Offutt [their employer] that not having been able to purchase a boat in Beardstown, he had concluded to build one on the Sangamon River. Lincoln, Hanks, and Johnston were hired for that purpose at twelve dollars per month [about $225 per month in modern dollars],[2] and

---

[1] Writing in July 1860, Mr. Scripps is hopeful about the November election.

[2] Modern dollars are editor's estimates of equivalent amounts for year 2007.

going into the woods, they got out the necessary timber and built a boat at the town of Sangamon—near where the Chicago, Alton, and St. Louis Railroad now crosses the Sangamon River—which they took to New Orleans upon the old contract. [They previously agreed with Mr. Offutt to transport and sell his produce there].

The writer has not been put in possession of any of the incidents connected with this trip. [Editor's Note: John Hanks, a crewmate on this flatboat trip of 1831, later claimed that Mr. Lincoln was appalled by an auction of slaves in New Orleans, and vowed to someday attack slavery. However, Mr. Lincoln never publicly commented, and Mr. Hanks, his cousin, was hardly impartial.[1] Nevertheless, in 1831, New Orleans was a center of slave trading, and Mr. Lincoln, age 22, saw *something*, although what is unclear.

Politics may also be at work. As a presidential candidate, Mr. Lincoln sought to soften his reputation as an antislavery firebrand, promising only to limit, not abolish slavery. In 1860, he would have been less than eager to confirm a story that suggested his heated reputation was well deserved.]

[Storekeeper]

It is sufficient for the present purpose, however, to know that so well did young Lincoln bear himself throughout [on the above journey]—so faithful in all the trusts reposed in him by his employer; so active, prompt, and efficient in all necessary labor; so cool, determined, and full of resources in the presence of danger—that before reaching New Orleans, Offutt [his employer] had become greatly attached to him and, on their return, engaged him to take the general charge of a store and mill in the village of New Salem, then in Sangamon, now in Menard County.

In July 1831, Lincoln was fairly installed in this new business. In those primitive times, the country merchant was a personage of vast consequence. He was made the repository of all the news of the surrounding settlements, and as he "took the [news]papers," he was able to post his customers, [keeping them informed] as to the affairs of state and the news of the world generally.

His acquirements in this last respect were as astounding to the country people as were those of Goldsmith's village schoolmaster[2]

---

[1]   Tarbell, *The Life of Abraham Lincoln*, I:58.

[2]   A scholarly character depicted by Oliver Goldsmith (1730-74), a popular novelist of village life in eighteenth-century England.

to the simple rustics [or country people of rural England]. His [Lincoln's] store was a place of common resort for the people on rainy days, and at those periods of the year when farmwork was not pressing, and nearly always on Saturday afternoons. There [at these gatherings] all the topics of the neighborhood and of the times were discussed, the merchant usually bearing the leading part; and all disputed points of past history or of current events were always referred to him as the ultimate tribunal for decision. His word and opinion in these respects were supreme, never disputed, and triumphantly repeated by the fortunate first-hearers at all casual meetings with neighbors, and at all the little neighborhood gatherings at which the oracle [Lincoln] was not present.

Young Lincoln's acquirements and natural gifts most admirably fitted him for the distinction awarded to men engaged in his new occupation. He had read a few books, as we have seen; had been twice to New Orleans; and otherwise had observed a good deal of

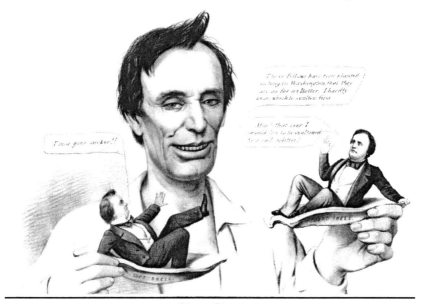

River Giant

Political cartoons of 1860 played upon Mr. Lincoln's early life on frontier rivers. Here he devours "clamshells" of the divided opposition. The cartoon mocks Washington insiders.

Image courtesy of Library of Congress.

the world, treasuring up [or recalling for his audience's pleasure]
whatever he had seen faithfully in his memory. He had an unfailing
fund of anecdote; he was an admirable talker—sharp, witty, good-
humored—and possessed also of an accommodating spirit which always led him to exert himself for the entertainment of his friends,
as well as to be ever ready to do any of them a kind and neighborly
turn when his assistance was needed.

In a very little time, he had become the most popular man in
the neighborhood. His new acquaintances respected him for his up-
rightness, honored him for his intelligence, admired him for his genial and social qualities; and loved him him for that deep, earnest
sympathy which he ever manifested for those who were unfortu-
nate in their enterprises, or who were overtaken by some great sorrow. How much they confided in him, honored and loved him, will
be seen a little further on.

[First War]

[Editor's Note: Then, as now, American presidential candidates routinely
touted their military experience. In 1860, Abraham Lincoln had incentive to
follow tradition: His opponents pummeled him for past antiwar activities.
(See Chapter Six.) Also, the antiwar movement of the era routinely deflected
criticism by supporting senior military officers for president—John C. Frémont in 1856, Winfield Scott in 1852, and Zachary Taylor in 1848.

Nevertheless, Abraham Lincoln directed his biographer, Mr. Scripps, to
make an untraditional presentation. Young Mr. Lincoln, age 23, appears below as a sincere, but hapless antihero during an Indian war. The tale wavers
between demonizing the opposing natives and acknowledging their
grievances. Other politicians of the era usually endorsed unqualified bias
against Indians. Mr. Scripps, though, still inflates Mr. Lincoln's minor service
against a local chief into a grand Napoleonic saga.]

Early in the following spring (1832) the Black Hawk War broke
out in the northwestern part of the State [Illinois]. The previous
year, a part of the tribes of the Sauk[1] and Fox Indians had recrossed the Mississippi [River] from its western bank [moving from
present-day Iowa into Illinois], and taken possession of their old
town on Rock River, a few miles above its mouth, and about four
miles from where the city of Rock Island is now situated.

---

[1] Spelled *Sac* in the 1860 text.

The Indian title to the lands in that vicinity had been extinguished by a treaty made [by the United States] with the chiefs of the Sauk and Fox Nations at St. Louis in 1804. Which treaty [i.e., *that* treaty] was afterwards confirmed by a portion of the tribes in 1815, and by another portion in 1816.

Black Hawk [an Indian leader in northwestern Illinois] always denied the validity of these treaties, and in fact, of all the treaties made by his people with the whites. In the War of 1812, he had cooperated with the British army [against the United States] and had conceived an unconquerable hatred of the Americans.[1]

[In 1831] the lands on which the great town of his nation was situated had recently been surveyed and brought into market, and a number of white settlers had gone upon them. This aroused the enmity of the old chieftain, and taking with him his women and children, and as many warriors as he could inspire with the same feeling, he returned to his former haunts, took possession of the ancient metropolis of his people, ordered the white settlers away, killed their stock, unroofed their houses, pulled down their fences, and cut up their growing grain.

News of these outrages reaching Governor Reynolds,[2] [the latter mobilized the military]. At his request, General Gaines[3] [commander of the U.S. Army's Western Military Department] proceeded at once to Rock Island. Becoming convinced that Black Hawk meditated war on the settlers, General Gaines called upon Governor Reynolds for a small force

Library of Congress

Black Hawk

---

[1] Black Hawk (1767-1838) was born in colonial times under British rule.

[2] John Reynolds (1788-1865) was governor of Illinois, 1830-34.

[3] Edmund P. Gaines (1777-1849) was a renown Indian fighter.

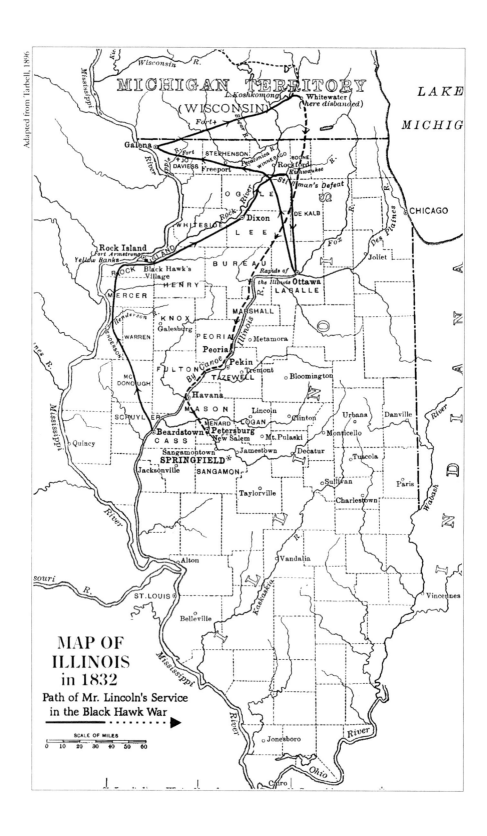

Adapted from Tarbell, 1896

MICHIGAN TERRITORY
(WISCONSIN)

L. Koshkonong
Whitewater
(here disbanded)

LAKE
MICHIG

Fort +

Galena

Fort
JO
DAVIESS
Freeport

STEPHENSON
Pecatonica R.

WINNEBAGO
Rockford
Kishwaukee

BOONE

St. Vllman's Defeat

CHICAGO

O G LE

DE KALB

Dixon

WHITESIDE
LEE

Rock Island
Fort Armstrong
Yellow Banks

ROCK ISLAND

Rock River

Fox R.

Des Plaines R.

Joliet

ROCK
Black Hawk's
Village

BUREAU

Rapids of
the Illinois Ottawa
LASALLE

HENRY

MERCER

Henderson R.

KNOX
Galesburg

MARSHALL

Metamora

WARREN

PEORIA
Peoria

Illinois R.

I N D I A N A

MC
DONOUGH

FULTON

By Canoe

Pekin
Tremont
TAZEWELL

Bloomington

SCHUYLER

Havana

MASON

Lincoln
LOGAN

Clinton

Urbana

Danville

Wabash River

Quincy

Beardstown
CASS

MENARD
Petersburg
New Salem
Jamestown

Mt. Pulaski

Monticello

Tuscola

Paris

Sangamontown
SPRINGFIELD*
Jacksonville SANGAMON

Decatur

Sullivan

Charlestown

Mississippi R.

Taylorville

souri R.

Alton

Vandalia

ST. LOUIS

Belleville

Kaskaskia R.

Vincennes

MAP OF
ILLINOIS
in 1832

Path of Mr. Lincoln's Service
in the Black Hawk War

SCALE OF MILES
0 10 20 30 40 50 60

Mississippi River

Jonesboro

Ohio River

Cairo

of mounted volunteers [recruited from people living in Illinois]. These were soon in the field and in a short time, together with a few regular troops, appeared before Black Hawk's town. The latter [the Indian chief], with his women and children and fighting men, retreated [westward into Iowa] across the Mississippi [River] without firing a gun. The volunteers destroyed the town and encamped upon the Mississippi, on the site of the present city of Rock Island.

Black Hawk, anticipating that the troops would follow him to the west side of the river, came into Fort Armstrong [on the east, or Illinois side, of the Mississippi River] and sued for peace. [In 1831] a treaty was then made, in which it was stipulated that Black Hawk's people should remain, forever after, on the west side of the river, never to recross it without permission of the president of the United States, or the governor of Illinois.*[1]

This treaty proved to be but an Indian's stratagem. Black Hawk's sole object in making it was to gain time in order to perfect his preparations. He was fully bent upon war, and early in the following spring [1832] he recrossed the Mississippi in force, moving up the valley of the Rock River to the country of the Pottawatomies and the Winnebagoes [two Indian tribes], whom he hoped to make his allies. [Black Hawk led about a thousand people, but not all warriors. Many were women, children, and old men.]

As soon as apprised of these facts, Governor Reynolds issued a call for four regiments of volunteers [totaling 4,000 soldiers]. Among the earliest in his neighborhood to enroll himself for this service, was young Lincoln. A company [a group of a hundred soldiers] was formed in New Salem, and to his own great surprise, though doubtless not to the surprise of anyone else, Lincoln was chosen captain. This was the first evidence he had ever received of popularity among his acquaintances, and he has often said later in life (and since he has won the distinction of a leading man in the nation) that no other success ever gave him so much unalloyed satisfaction.

---

[1] [Original footnote:] *Ford's History of Illinois*, page 108, *et seq.*

The volunteers [to fight Black Hawk's Indians] rendezvoused at Beardstown [Illinois]. Here Lincoln's company joined its regiment [a larger military unit with a thousand soldiers], and after a few days of rapid marching, the scene of conflict was reached.

[Beyond a brief summary] it is not the intention to give an account of this war. It was of short duration. Black Hawk took the field early in April [1832]. In the last days of the following July, the decisive battle of the Bad Axe was fought, which put an end to the war; and a few days thereafter, Black Hawk and his principal braves—who had escaped the bullet and the bayonet—were prisoners of war at Fort Armstrong on Rock Island.

But short as it was, the Indians showed themselves to be courageous, desperate, and merciless. Their war parties traversed the whole country from Rock Island [on the Iowa border] to the neighborhood of Chicago, and from the Illinois River into the Territory of Wisconsin. They occupied every grove; waylaid every road; hung around every settlement; picked off many of the settlers without regard to age, sex, or condition; and attacked every small party of white men that attempted to penetrate the country.*[1]

[Nevertheless, Mr. Lincoln's military service was brief.] The first levy of volunteers was called out for but thirty days. At the end of that time, they were disbanded at Ottawa [Illinois] without having seen the enemy.

When the troops were disbanded, most of them returned home. Lincoln, however, had gone out for the war [he wanted to serve until its end]; and a new levy being called for, he again volunteered and served as a private [giving up his captaincy, and entering the lowest rank for thirty days]. A second time his regiment was disbanded, and again he volunteered. When his third term of service had expired, the war was about concluded, and he returned home.

Having lost his horse, near where the town of Janesville, Wisconsin, now stands, he went down Rock River to Dixon in a canoe. Thence he crossed the country on foot to Peoria, where he again took canoe to a point on the Illinois River within forty miles of

---

[1]   [Original footnote:] *Ford's History of Illinois*, page 123.

home [New Salem in central Illinois]. The latter distance he accomplished on foot, having been in active service nearly three months. [The total journey home was over 200 miles. His entire military service traversed perhaps 600 miles or more.]

We have been told by men who were with Lincoln during this campaign, that he was always prompt and energetic in the performance of duty, never shrinking from danger or hardship; that he was a universal favorite, the best talker, the best storyteller, and the best at a wrestling match or a footrace in the whole army. He still owns the land in Iowa on which his own warrants [or grants of public land] for this service were located.

[Editor's Note: Thus ended Mr. Lincoln's inglorious military career. An earnest youth—who dreamed of emulating George Washington—never saw combat, suffered demotion, lost his horse, hiked home, and was only "best talker." Although Mr. Lincoln later told the tale with humor, the disappointment was real. For the Black Hawk War of 1832 was covered by national news reporters; but for fate, a young adventurer might have been the famous war hero of his dreams.

However, nearly thirty years later, a wiser Mr. Lincoln had good reason for modesty. In 1860, his main opponent for the presidency, Stephen Douglas, accused him of inciting armed conflict over slavery. In reply, Mr. Lincoln's campaign biography rejects violence. A hapless military record helps confirm his pacifism.

However, unbeknown to the candidate, an eerie omen had marked his last day as a soldier. In 1832, a junior army officer, Lieutenant Robert Anderson (1805-70), quietly discharged Private Abraham Lincoln back into civilian life. Three decades later, in April 1861, the new President Lincoln would find himself desperately trying to save the same officer from besieging pro-slavery rebels. Then Major Anderson was the heroic U.S. commander of Fort Sumter, South Carolina. The surrounding rebels opened fire with artillery, thwarting Mr. Lincoln's attempt to resupply the fort, and beginning the American Civil War.]

Library of Congress

Robert Anderson

Chapter Four
Merchant—Surveyor—Legislator—Lawyer

Lincoln a Candidate for the Legislature—The Vote of New Salem—Merchant
Again—Studies English Grammar—Deputy Surveyor—Elected to the Legislature—Douglas's Opinion of Lincoln—The True Test of Genius—Studies
Law and Removes to Springfield—A Reminiscence—Lincoln's First Speech
—Political Complexion of Illinois for Twenty Years—Lincoln Recognized as
a Leader—Twice He Receives the Vote of His Party for Speaker—Summary
of His Career in the State Legislature.

P rior to the adoption of the present Constitution of Illinois in
1847, elections for state officers and members of the legislature were held on the first Monday in August—for the former once in four years, for the latter once in every two years. Lincoln's return to New Salem [from the Black Hawk War of 1832]
was, therefore, but a few days before the election of that year for
members of the legislature. [He returned in mid-July 1832.]

The system of nominating candidates for office by county and
state conventions had not then been introduced into Illinois. Indeed, party lines and party designations were at that time scarcely
known in the State. There were "Clay Men," "Jackson Men,"
"Adams Men," "Crawford Men," and so on,[1] but no clearly defined
party creeds around which men of similar views rallied to make
common cause against those holding opposite opinions. [As individuals without parties] men announced themselves as candidates
for the various elective offices. It was a very rare circumstance that
a contest for an office was narrowed down to two candidates. More
frequently a half-dozen eager aspirants contested the prize.

The County of Sangamon [Illinois] was entitled to four members
in the lower branch of the legislature, and there were at the time of
Lincoln's return more than twice that number of candidates.

---

[1] These are supporters of presidential candidates Henry Clay of Kentucky,
Andrew Jackson of Tennessee, John Quincy Adams of Massachusetts, and Wil-
liam H. Crawford of Georgia. All ran for president in 1824, a contest won by
John Quincy Adams, the son of the American Revolutionary John Adams.

Andrew Jackson (1767-1845)
U.S. President, 1829-37

President Jackson was a popular war hero. Young Mr. Lincoln preferred the opposing Whig Party and its policies for economic development.

Library of Congress

Among the number were some of the ablest, best known, and most popular men of the county, of whom may be mentioned John T. Stuart, afterwards representative in Congress; Colonel E. D. Taylor; Peter Cartwright, the famous, eccentric Methodist preacher; and others of considerable note. These gentlemen had been in the field some time before the return of Lincoln; [they] had canvassed the county thoroughly, defining their position on local and other questions, and obtaining promises of support.

[Yet] Lincoln had no sooner returned than he was urgently besought by his friends at New Salem to enter the lists for the legislature against this array of strong men and old citizens. These entreaties continued from day to day, together with the cordial reception he had just received at the hands of all his old acquaintances. [They] induced him, against his better judgment, to give a reluctant assent, knowing very well that, under the circumstances, his election was entirely out of the question.

It will be remembered that the county [Sangamon, Illinois] was a large one; that he had lived in it only from July [1831] to the following April [1832]; that he had but few acquaintances outside of the precinct of New Salem; and that the election was so near at hand as to deprive him of the opportunity of visiting other portions of the county, and making himself known to the people.

Nevertheless, when the election came off [in August 1832], he was but a few votes behind the successful candidates. His own precinct—New Salem—gave him 277 votes in a poll of 284 [or 98 percent];[1] and this, too, in the face of his avowed preferences for Mr. Clay [an underdog presidential candidate]; and notwithstanding the same precinct at the presidential election three months later gave a majority of 115 for General Jackson [overwhelming the losing Mr. Clay by about 40-percentage points].

[Editor's Note: In 1832, President Andrew Jackson, a former army general, won a landslide reelection over U.S. Senator Henry Clay of Kentucky. Mr. Lincoln, a political novice at age 23, also lost his legislative race, but easily won more votes in his precinct than the famous Mr. Clay. (See page 153.)]

The result of this election—though practically a defeat—was, all circumstances considered, a most brilliant triumph [for Mr. Lincoln], clearly presaging success in any future trial he might make. And never since that day has Mr. Lincoln been beaten in any direct vote of the people.

Having received such generous treatment at the hands of his New Salem friends, Mr. Lincoln resolved to make the place his permanent home. He was wholly without means, and at a loss as to what he should try to do. At one time, he had almost concluded to learn the trade of a blacksmith. Those who discerned in the young man qualities which he had not yet suspected himself to be the possessor of, urged him to turn his attention to the profession of law; but he always met suggestions of this character with objections based upon his lack of education.

While yet in a quandary as to the future, he was very unexpectedly met with a proposition to purchase on credit, in connection with another man as poor as himself, an old stock of goods. The offer was accepted, and forthwith he was installed at the head of a village store. It is needless to recount the difficulties which beset him as a merchant. It is enough to say that after a manly struggle with certain adverse circumstances for which he was not responsi-

---

[1] A later study tallied 277 of 300 votes, or 92 percent—still impressive. Ida Tarbell, *The Early Life of Abraham Lincoln* (New York: McClure, 1896), p. 158.

Self-Made Man
In his 20s, Abraham Lincoln educated himself by the flickering light of a fireplace.
Above is an artist's interpretation from the nineteenth-century.

ble, he relinquished the business, finding himself encumbered with debt—which he afterwards paid to the last farthing. While engaged in this business he received the appointment of postmaster of New Salem, the profits of the office being too insignificant to make his politics an objection.

[Editor's Note: In 1832, Mr. Lincoln backed the losing Henry Clay for president, but yet the victorious Andrew Jackson appointed him U.S. Postmaster for New Salem on May 7, 1833. The postmaster's job, though, was only part-time work. He had little to do after he left the above store.]

Again thrown out of employment, Mr. Lincoln now turned his attention more than ever to books. He read everything that fell in his way; he kept himself well posted in national politics. He accustomed himself to write out his views on various topics of general interest, though not for the public eye; and realizing in these exercises the importance of a correct knowledge of English grammar, he took up that study for the first time.

[Surveyor]

[Editor's Note: Abraham Lincoln seldom made his political disputes into personal ones. The below passage describes his early friendship with a local official of the Democratic Party who later became a proslavery partisan.]

About this period [circa 1833] he made the acquaintance of John Calhoun, then living in Springfield [Illinois], and afterwards notorious for his efforts to maintain Democratic supremacy in Kansas,[1] and as president of the Lecompton Constitutional Convention [which, in 1857, proposed a proslavery regime for Kansas].

[In 1833, though, John Calhoun offered a job to the struggling Mr. Lincoln, age 24.] Mr. Calhoun was then County Surveyor for Sangamon County. The great influx of immigrants before spoken of, and the consequent active entry of the government lands [for new farms], gave him more business in the way of establishing corners, and tracing boundary lines than he could well attend to.

[Editor's Note: The county surveyor was an important official who mapped boundaries of farms carved from the frontier. Accuracy and honesty were essential. Errors resulted in lawsuits and loss of land by settlers. Mr. Lincoln's father may have lost land in Kentucky due to a defective survey.]

Conceiving a liking for Mr. Lincoln, Calhoun offered to depute to him that portion of the work contiguous to New Salem. Lincoln had no knowledge of surveying, or of the science on which it is based; but he was now too much absorbed by a desire for improvement to decline a position which, while securing a livelihood, would enable him to increase his acquirements. He accepted the kind proffer of Mr. Calhoun, contrived to procure a compass and chain [instruments for measuring land], set himself down to the study of *Flint* and *Gibson* [two textbooks on surveying], and in a very short time took the field as a surveyor.

Mr. Lincoln never forgot or ceased to be grateful for this kindness. Although he and Mr. Calhoun were ever afterwards political opponents, he always treated him fairly, placed the most charitable construction possible upon his actions, and never lost an opportunity to do a kindly act, either for him or his family.

[Birth of a Statesman]

In the summer of 1834, Mr. Lincoln [age 25] was again a candidate for the legislature. He had now become acquainted with the people throughout the county [Sangamon]; and although they had not seen enough of him to have learned to appreciate him quite as highly as the people of New Salem precinct, nevertheless he was

---

[1] *Democratic supremacy* refers to the Democratic Party of the 1850s.

this time elected by an overwhelming majority, and by the largest vote cast for any candidate.

Up to this period, and indeed for the two years after [until 1836], Mr. Lincoln was not aware that he possessed any faculty for public speaking. His acquaintances knew him to be an admirable talker, full of original thought; a close reasoner united to a matchless gift of illustration [i.e., he told colorful parables]; and from their eager desire to get him into the legislature, it is more than probable that they believed he would there develop into a forcible and ready debater. Whatever they had known him to undertake he had done well; and they therefore had faith in his success, should he enter this new and untried field of effort.

In one of his memorable debates with Stephen A. Douglas in 1858 [during their contest for U.S. senator from Illinois], the latter, in alluding to the early experiences in life, as well as to the later efforts of his opponent, said: *"Lincoln is one of those peculiar men who perform with admirable skill everything they undertake."* Douglas had known and watched him closely for a quarter of a century—watched him not as an admirer and friend, but as a political opponent whom he always dreaded to encounter, and whose failure

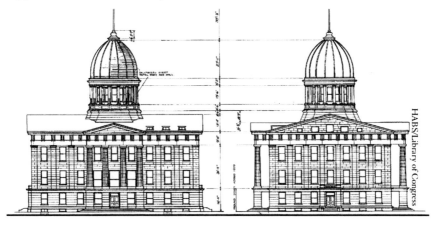

Old State House, Springfield
As a young legislator in the 1830s, Mr. Lincoln helped bring the state capital of Illinois to Springfield. Two decades later, he gave his "House Divided" speech in the city's Old State House. The event put him on a path to the presidency.

in anything would have given him sincere gratification—and this
[praise of Lincoln's ability] was the conclusion to which he had
been forced to come, contrary to his wishes.

[For] to be able to rise with the occasion, and to never fall below it, is one of the surest marks of genius; and we have the authority of the man [Stephen Douglas]—who, of all men in the
world, is the least likely to be biased in Mr. Lincoln's favor—for
saying that he has never failed to come up to this standard.

[Legislator and Law Student]

The trait of character to which Mr. Douglas thus bore reluctant
testimony, had been early remarked by Lincoln's friends. It was not
wonderful, therefore, that they had implicit faith in him [as their
state legislator]. That although [Mr. Lincoln was] young and wholly
inexperienced in legislation, they cheerfully confided their interests
to his keeping. For in [knowing] his past life, they had the strongest
possible guarantee that in this new sphere, he would make himself
"master of the situation," and fully equal to all of its duties.

But in the session [of the legislature] of 1834-35, Mr. Lincoln
did not attempt to make a speech [in a major floor debate]. [Yet] he
was faithful in his attendance; watchful of the interests of his constituents; acquired the confidence of his fellow members as a man
of sound judgment and patriotic purposes; and in this manner he
wielded a greater influence in shaping and controlling legislation
than many of the noisy declaimers and most frequent speakers of
the body. His constituents were satisfied—so well satisfied indeed,
that they reelected him in 1836, again in 1838, and again in 1840,
and would have continued electing him, had he desired it. But by
this time, as we shall presently see, his circumstances and position
were greatly changed, and there were higher duties before him.

During the canvass [or election campaign] for the legislature in
1834, Mr. Lincoln was thrown considerably into the company of
Honorable John T. Stuart of Springfield, then a candidate for reelection. The latter gentleman, with his accustomed penetration [a
shrewd ability to assess a man's character], was not long in discovering in his retiring and unassuming companion, powers of mind,

which if properly developed, could not fail to confer distinction upon their possessor.

To Lincoln's great surprise, Mr. Stuart warmly urged him to study law. Mr. Stuart was a gentleman of education, an able lawyer, and in every respect one of the foremost men of the State. Advice of this character, tendered by one so competent to give it, could not be otherwise than gratifying to a young man as yet unknown to fame outside of New Salem precinct, and being accompanied by a generous offer to loan him whatever books he might need, Lincoln resolved to follow it. As soon as the election was over [in August 1834], he took home with him a few books from the law library of Mr. Stuart, and entered upon their study in his usually earnest way. When the legislature met in the following December, the law books were laid aside, but were resumed again immediately after the adjournment [on February 13, 1835].

In the autumn of 1836, Mr. Lincoln was admitted to the bar [the official association of lawyers], and on the fifteenth day of the following April, having formed a co-partnership with his old friend Stuart, he removed to Springfield [from New Salem] and entered upon his professional career.

[The Simple Life]

During all this time—that is, from his acceptance of the post of deputy-surveyor [for New Salem in 1833] under Calhoun until he removed to Springfield in 1837—he supported himself by occasional jobs of surveying. Of course, he was compelled to live as cheaply as possible; to dress as he had always done before, and always has done since, in plain, simple garb; and to study at night by the light of the fire, candles being a luxury he could not then afford. Yet, he was always buoyant, enjoyed life, and never once fancied that his condition was otherwise than an enviable one.

His most severe annoyances grew out of his rare gifts as a talker. His friends *would* come to see him and to hear him talk, and whenever a stranger sojourned for a day or more in New Salem, these friends could not forego the gratification of showing off the fine points of the village favorite.

Tarbell, 1907

First Law Office
In 1837, the novice lawyer Abraham Lincoln, age 28, became junior partner in a two-person firm. Decades later, his upstairs office became a furniture store. (Second from right.) His modest start inspired generations of young lawyers.

Apropos to incidents of this character, is the following, related by Honorable Richard Yates, the distinguished Republican candidate for governor of Illinois [in the then coming election of November 1860],[1] in a speech delivered at Springfield, on the seventh of June last, to a meeting composed of Mr. Lincoln's old friends and neighbors, many of whom had known him intimately at the time referred to.

Said Mr. Yates:

"I recollect the first time I ever saw Old Abe, and I have a great mind to tell you, though I don't know that I ought to. *['Yes, go on—go on.']*[2] It was more than a quarter of a century ago [circa 1833]. *[A voice: 'He was "Young Abe" then.']* I was down at Salem with a friend, who remarked to me one day, 'I'll go over and introduce you to a fine young fellow we have here —a smart, genial, active young fellow—*and we'll be certain to have a good talk.*'

---

[1]   Messrs. Scripps and Lincoln wrote this book in June and July 1860.

[2]   Italicized responses are those of the audience and appear in the 1860 text.

"I consented, and he took me down to a collection of four or five houses, and looking over the way, I saw a young man partly lying or resting on a cellar door, intently engaged in reading. My friend took me up and introduced me to young Lincoln, and I tell you, as he rose up, I would not have shot at him *then* for a president. *[Laughter.]* **[Editor's Note: Mr. Lincoln seldom fussed about his appearance. His hair and clothes were often less than perfect.]**

"Well, after some pleasant conversation—*for Lincoln talked then just as he does now*—we all went up to dinner. You know, we all lived in a very plain way in those times. The house was a rough log house, with a puncheon floor[1] and clapboard roof, and might have been built, like Solomon's Temple, 'without the sound of hammer or nail,' for there was no iron in it. *[Laughter.]*

"The old lady, whose house it was, soon provided us with a dinner, the principal ingredient of which was a great bowl of milk, which she handed to each. Somehow in serving Lincoln, there was a mistake made, and his bowl tipped up, and the bowl and milk rolled over the floor. The good old lady was in deep distress, and exclaimed, 'Oh, dear me! That's all my fault.'

"Lincoln picked up the bowl in the best natured way in the world, remarking to her, 'Aunt Lizzy, we'll not discuss whose fault it was; only if it don't worry you, it don't worry me.' *[Laughter and applause.]* The old lady was comforted, and gave him another bowl of milk. *[Renewed laughter.]*

"My friend Green [William G. *Greene*],[2] who introduced me to Lincoln, told me the first time he ever saw him, he was in the Sangamon River [on April 19, 1831], with his pants rolled up some five feet, more or less *[great merriment]*, trying to pilot a flatboat over a mill dam. The boat had got so full of water that it was very difficult to manage, and almost impossible to get it over the dam.

"Lincoln finally contrived to get her prow over so that it projected a few feet [dangling over the edge of the dam], and there it stood. But he then invented a new way of bailing a flatboat:

---

[1] A crude wooden floor made with split timbers, the flat side up.

[2] A banker in 1860, but a clerk in the same store as Mr. Lincoln in 1831.

He bored a hole through the bottom to let the water run out, and then corked her up, and she launched right over. *[Great laughter.]* I think the captain who proved himself so fitted to navigate the broad-horn[1] over the dam, is no doubt the man who is to stand upon the deck of the old ship, 'The Constitution,' and guide her safely over the billows and breakers that surround her." *[Enthusiastic and prolonged applause.]*

[Early Debates]

It has been already stated that Lincoln was a *working* member of the legislature at the session of 1834-35, but did not attempt the *role* of a speaker. [By which is meant that he never formally debated major issues along party lines. At the time, candidates ran as popular individuals, rather than as nominees of political parties.]

[Elections soon changed.] The convention system [by which the Democratic Party formally nominated candidates] had been introduced into Illinois by Stephen A. Douglas in 1834; and about that time the opponents of the administration [of Democratic President Andrew Jackson] began calling themselves "Whigs," and laying the foundation of a party organization. Party spirit soon began to run high, and political discussions between leading men of the two parties were of frequent occurrence. [Mr. Lincoln became a Whig, favoring more government-backed economic development.]

Lincoln's first speech [in a formal partisan debate] was made during the canvass for the legislature in 1836. The candidates had met at Springfield by appointment for the purpose of a public discussion. A large concourse of citizens had assembled in the courthouse to listen to the speeches. Ninian W. Edwards,[2] then a Whig, led off. He was followed by Dr. [Jacob] Early,[3] who was regarded as one of the most effective debaters on the Democratic side in the State. [Dr.] Early was severe upon Edwards, and the latter was desirous of making an immediate rejoinder.

---

[1]   A *broad-horn* is a short, but bulky flatboat.

[2]   In 1839, Ninian Edwards introduced his sister-in-law, Mary Todd, to Mr. Lincoln. The latter two were married three years later, in 1842.

[3]   Captain Jacob M. Early was one of Lincoln's commanding officers during the Black Hawk War of 1832.

But Early's speech had aroused Lincoln. His [Lincoln's] name was the next on the program, and telling Edwards to be patient, he arose to reply. Although embarrassed at the beginning, his exordium [or introduction] gave indications of what was to come. He began in that slow and deliberate manner which is still one of his marked characteristics as a speaker, succinctly and lucidly stating the principles of the two parties, carefully laying down his premises, and weaving a network of facts and deductions around his adversary, from which escape was utterly impossible.

In less than five minutes, all traces of embarrassment had disappeared. As he warmed with his subject, his tall form grew proudly erect, his gray eye[s] burning and flashing with an intensity never witnessed before, and all his features in full play—now mantling with humor, as some well-aimed shaft of ridicule penetrated and disclosed a weak place in his opponent's argument. And [in another moment, his face was] now glowing with an honest indignation, as he laid bare the sophisms and misrepresentations with which it [his foe's position] abounded.

When he [Lincoln] sat down, his reputation was made. Not only had he achieved a signal victory over the acknowledged champion of Democracy [the then nickname of the Democratic Party], but he had placed himself, by a single effort, in the very front rank of able and eloquent debaters. The surprise of his audience was only equaled by their enthusiasm; and of all the surprised people on that memorable occasion, perhaps no one was more profoundly astonished than Lincoln himself. In the election which followed, [Dr.] Early was defeated, and with him, every Democratic candidate on the ticket—a result to which Lincoln's masterly efforts before the people largely contributed.

[Editor's Note: The above narrative is vague because intangible disputes about personal character, style, and integrity dominated debates in frontier Illinois. On policy matters, little separated the young political parties. Both Whigs and Democrats in Illinois supported massive government spending— and borrowing—to construct railroads and canals. Other States joined the spending binge, creating a speculative bubble which collapsed in 1837, only a year after the above debate. The resulting recession increased political bickering. Mr. Lincoln's Whigs still supported "internal improvements," but local Democrats, guided by their national leaders, increasingly opposed them.]

In the following December [1836], Lincoln took his seat a second time in the legislature [as part of the Whig minority]. It is proper to state here that Illinois, until of late years [in the 1850s], has always been strongly Democratic—it gave its electoral vote [for president] to Jackson in 1832; to Van Buren in 1836 and in 1840; to Polk in 1844; to Cass in 1848; and to Pierce in 1852.

[Editor's Note: Illinois usually voted for the winner in presidential elections, including Democrats Andrew Jackson, Martin Van Buren, James Polk, and Franklin Pierce; only Lewis Cass lost nationally. Illinois was a good bellwether, because it had settlers from both North and South.]

During these twenty years [1832-52], with the exception of a part of Governor [Joseph] Duncan's term, who was elected as a Jackson man [in 1834], but identified himself with the Whig Party before the close of his administration, all the state offices and the state legislature were in the possession of the Democratic Party. The whole responsibility of the state government devolved upon that party.

The Whigs in the legislature, as a party, had no power to inaugurate a policy of their own [because they were a perpetual minority]. Their hands were effectually tied. The most they could do was, in cases in which their opponents differed among themselves on questions of policy, to throw their votes on the side that seemed to them the least mischievous.

Such was the condition of things when Mr. Lincoln entered the legislature in 1834 [in the Whig minority]. It had not altered in any respect when he took his seat a second time in that body in 1836, nor indeed at any subsequent period while he remained a member of it. During the session of 1836-37, he was recognized from the start as a leader of his party on the floor of the House [the junior chamber of the legislature], and made such a reputation for himself in that capacity, that both in 1838 and in 1840, he received the unanimous vote of his party friends for Speaker.

The details of state legislation afford but few matters of interest to the general reader, and for that reason it is not proposed to follow Mr. Lincoln through this portion of his career. It is enough to say on this head [or subject], that he was always watchful of the public interests; labored zealously and with great efficiency for whatever he believed would promote the welfare of the State; and opposed with untiring energy every measure that he thought would have an opposite tendency.

He entered the body [the Illinois House of Representatives] in 1834, the youngest member in it [at age 25], with a fame that had not extended beyond the limits of his own county. [He was] distrustful of himself by reason of his lack of education; inexperienced in legislation; and having no knowledge of the arts and chicanery with which he would have to contend.

[Yet Mr. Lincoln served four terms in the Illinois House.] He left it in 1840,[1] by common consent, the ablest man in it. [He was] the recognized leader of his party in the House and in the State; his name familiar as a household word from Cairo to Galena, and from the Wabash to the Mississippi [respectively the towns and rivers bordering Illinois]. And [he retired] with a reputation for honesty and integrity which not even the bitterest of his political opponents had the hardihood to asperse.

Transition

A prolonged economic recession, the Crash of 1837-40, prompted Mr. Lincoln's early retirement from the state legislature. In an era of shrinking budgets, critics derided his quixotic advocacy of better schools and transportation. Skeptics also scorned his lonely first protest against slavery. (See page 110.)

Mr. Lincoln's woes coincided with a fateful transition. In scarcely a dozen years, his activist Whig Party disintegrated, while a conservative Democratic Party swept the nation as a staunch ally of slavery.

The frustrated Mr. Lincoln, still only 32 years old, returned to practice law in small-town Springfield. Ever honest, he never exploited his legislative office for personal gain. He was stone broke and turned to the mundane task of earning a living. By doing so, he would create a new legend as the proverbial country lawyer.

---

[1] Mr. Lincoln was last *reelected* in 1840. He left the legislature in 1841.

Chapter Five
[Attorney at Law]

Resolves to Devote Himself to His Profession [as a Lawyer]—The Presidential
Canvass of 1840—Is Placed on the Electoral Ticket—First Contests with
Douglas—The Law Again: Some of Lincoln's Characteristics as a Lawyer—
His Marriage—The Canvass of 1844—Is Again Placed on the Electoral
Ticket—Discussions with Calhoun (of Kansas Notoriety)—His Speeches on
the Tariff—Speeches in Indiana.

On retiring from the legislature [in 1841], it was the intention of Mr. Lincoln to devote himself exclusively to the
labors of his profession [as a lawyer]. His own convictions
on the questions which divided parties were deeply rooted and im-
movable.

[Editor's Note: Economics, not slavery, then dominated politics. Mr. Lincoln's Whig Party favored more government-backed economic development.
Whigs also sought a tariff, or tax, to restrict foreign-made products, and to
protect American workers and industries. The Democratic Party opposed
these policies, but won most elections in Illinois. Mr. Lincoln's Whigs faded.]

His party in the State [Illinois] was in a hopeless minority.
There seemed but small opportunity for a man of his views to succeed in politics, while the qualities that he had by this time developed [in the law], insured both an honorable fame and a lucrative
income in his profession. To this he now turned, with all the
earnestness of his nature, and with a firm resolve to win laurels in
it worth the wearing.

But he was not permitted long to give his exclusive attention to
professional pursuits.[1] The groundswell of that political revolution,
which in 1840 carried the Whig Party into power in the national
government [by electing William H. Harrison as president], had no
sooner been felt, than there was a universal desire awakened
among the Whigs of Illinois to make one more effort to carry the
State over to the Whig column [in the same election of 1840].

Mr. Lincoln was assigned a place on the electoral ticket [pledged
for Mr. Harrison for president in the Electoral College]—a position

---

[1] The chronology is askew here. He focused on practicing law *after* 1840.

which he accepted with reluctance, but which he filled with great zeal and ability.[1] In that memorable canvass, he repeatedly met Mr. [Stephen] Douglas on the stump.

[Mr. Douglas, a Democrat, was a future opponent for U.S. senator and the White House. In 1840, he and Mr. Lincoln were state legislators and debated for opposing presidential candidates.] And it is no disparagement to that gentleman [Douglas] to say that then, as in later years, Mr. Lincoln proved himself to be immeasurably his superior—superior in logic, in argument, in resources as a debater, in broad and comprehensive views of national policy, in fairness, and in gentlemanly courtesy towards his competitor.

After the election of that year, Mr. Lincoln returned to his professional duties [as a lawyer]. He had now obtained a reputation at the bar which placed him in the front rank of the many able and profound jurists of the State. His services were eagerly sought in almost every case of importance; and perhaps no lawyer in Illinois or any other State has been more uniformly successful in the cases which he has undertaken.

It is one of the peculiarities of Mr. Lincoln as a lawyer, that he holds himself bound in honor and in conscience, having accepted a fee, to thoroughly master the case of his client. In this regard, he is

William Herndon (1818-91)
Best Law Partner

He worked with Mr. Lincoln for sixteen years, but was publicity shy. The campaign biography discreetly omits him. Mr. Herndon later wrote a bestselling memoir about his law partner.

McClure, 1901

---

[1] The U.S. Constitution requires that voters choose electors in an Electoral College, who then elect the president. In the modern era, these electors are nearly invisible to voters. In the 1840s, presidential electors ran full-throated campaigns for their candidates.

noted among his professional brethren for the greatness of his labors. He not only studies the side of his client, but that of his opponent also. Consequently he is never taken unawares, but has ample resources for whatever turn the ingenuity, skill, or learning of opposing counsel may give to the case.

To this peculiarity, in part, is owing the well-known fact that [his fellow lawyers will make him their leader] whenever Mr. Lincoln is employed in connection with other eminent counsel. Before the conclusion of the case, the sole management of it is almost invariably surrendered to him. Not by any ostentatious thrusting of himself forward is this position obtained, for nothing could be more foreign to Mr. Lincoln's manner, either at the bar or elsewhere. But [he becomes lead counsel by] proving himself to be more completely master of the case than his associates. The latter voluntarily award the position to him, and even insist upon his taking it.

Another peculiarity of Mr. Lincoln as a lawyer, is the fact that he is ever ready to give his assistance gratuitously to a poor client who has justice and right on his side. He has managed many such cases from considerations of a purely benevolent character, which he would not have undertaken for a fee. More than this, in cases of peculiar hardship, he has been known again and again [to secretly give a charitable donation to a poor client]—after throwing all of his power and ability as a lawyer into the management of the case without charge, or any other reward than the gratification of a noble nature on bidding his client *adieu.* And when receiving [from his client] his cordial thanks and the warm grasp of his hand, [Mr. Lincoln often quietly decides] to slip into his palm a five or a ten dollar bill *[about $110 to $220 in modern dollars]*, bidding him to say nothing about it, but to take heart and be hopeful.

Those who know him intimately will not be surprised at this relation, because it harmonizes well with his whole character; but so careful has he always been to conceal his charitable deeds, that the knowledge of such actions on his part is confined to those who have come into possession of it without his agency.

Mary Todd Lincoln (1818-81)
Wife

She married Abraham Lincoln for love.
Her family deemed him beneath her.

Library of Congress

In November 1842, Mr. Lincoln was united in marriage to Miss Mary Todd, daughter of Honorable Robert S. Todd of Lexington, Kentucky.[1] The fruits of this union are three sons now living, and one dead [who died in infancy]. The eldest [Robert], now in his seventeenth year, is a student at Exeter Academy, New Hampshire, preparatory to entering Harvard University. The other sons [Tad, or Thomas, age 7; and Willie, 10] are intelligent, promising lads.

Mrs. Lincoln is a lady of charming presence, of superior intelligence, of accomplished manners, and, in every respect, well fitted to adorn the position in which the election of her husband to the presidency will place her. The courtesies and hospitalities of the White House have never been more appropriately and gracefully dispensed than they will be during the administration of Mr. Lincoln.

[Protecting American Workers & Industries]

[Nonetheless, in the early 1840s, Mr. Lincoln was a lawyer, not a politician.] [Yet] from the retirement of his professional avocations, Mr. Lincoln was again called by his party to perform the labors of an elector for the State at large in the canvass of 1844 [a presidential election.] He entered upon the duties with his accustomed zeal, and with even more than his accustomed ability. [He was an elector pledged in the Electoral College for Henry Clay, a

---

[1]   Mr. Lincoln apparently did not inform his biographer about his first love, Ann Rutledge, who died tragically of a fever at age 22 in 1835.

second-time Whig nominee for president.][1] John Calhoun of Kansas notoriety,[2] then regarded as one of the ablest debaters on the Democratic side in the State [Illinois], was an elector-at-large on the [opposing] ticket of his party.

[Editor's Note: In the 1844 election, John Calhoun opposed Mr. Lincoln as a presidential elector, and was pledged to James Polk, a hawkish Democrat running for president against the Whig Henry Clay. During the campaign, Messrs. Lincoln and Calhoun debated their parties' respective policies on foreign trade. Mr. Lincoln, a Whig, advocated a higher tariff, or tax, to restrict foreign-made products from low-wage countries, and to protect American jobs and industries. Mr. Calhoun, a Democrat, opposed the higher tariff.]

Prosperity

"Resolved, *That a tariff of duties on imported goods, producing sufficient revenue for the payment of the necessary expenditures of the National Government, and so adjusted as to protect American industry, is indispensably necessary to the prosperity of the American people.*"

Abraham Lincoln, Delegate
Illinois Whig Party Convention
March 1, 1843

The meetings between these gentlemen in different parts of the State will not soon be forgotten by those who witnessed them. Calhoun exerted himself as he never had done before. Not even Douglas in his palmiest[3] days, ever bore aloft the Democratic standard more gallantly, or brought more strength of intellect to the defense of its principles. [The Democratic Party then favored importing foreign products over manufacturing products in America.]

But it was only the endeavor of a pygmy against an intellectual giant. His arguments were torn to tatters by Lincoln. His [Calhoun's] premises were left without foundation; and he had only the one resource of the demagogue left—to raise the party cry [appeal-

---

[1] In the 1840s, candidates for the Electoral College debated in their local communities for their respective presidential nominees.
[2] In 1857, John Calhoun helped draft a proslavery constitution for Kansas.
[3] *Palmy* is an antiquated word for *prosperous*.

ing to Illinois's historic ties to the Democratic Party of President Andrew Jackson], and to urge the faithful to a union of effort.

The issues of that day made the discussion of the tariff a prominent part of every political speech. It is believed by the most intelligent of Mr. Lincoln's hearers, that the doctrine of a tariff for the protection of home industry [i.e., the support of domestic manufacturing in the United States] has never received in this country a more exhaustive exposition, and a more triumphant vindication than in his speeches during that canvass.

Independence

"Permit me, fellow-citizens, to read the tariff plank of the Chicago platform [the policies of the presidential campaign] ..."

" '... we commend that policy of national exchanges which secures to working-men liberal wages; to agriculture remunerating prices; to mechanics and manufacturers adequate reward for their skill, labor, and enterprise; and to the nation commercial prosperity and independence.' "

Abraham Lincoln, President-elect
Speech at Pittsburgh, Pennsylvania
February 15, 1861

(It is to be regretted that the newspaper enterprise of Illinois at that day, did not embrace among its objects verbatim reports of public speeches. There is no trace of these efforts of Mr. Lincoln remaining, save in the recollection of those who were present at their delivery.)

Before the close of the campaign [of 1844], Mr. Lincoln accepted the earnest and oft-repeated invitation of leading Whigs in Indiana to visit that State. [Back home in Illinois, Whigs had already lost the early voting for the state legislature.] The result of the August election had demonstrated that Mr. Clay could not carry Illinois [in November's general election for president], while Indiana was considered debatable ground. The efforts of Mr. Lincoln—continuing through several weeks, and until the day of election—gave unbounded satisfaction to his political friends in Indiana, thousands of whom flocked to hear him at every appointment.

Chapter Six
In Congress

Unanimously Nominated for Congress—His Opponent, Peter Cartwright—
Unprecedented Majority—Enters Congress—A Brilliant Array of Great
Names—A Consistent Whig Record—The Mexican War—Lincoln Votes for
all the Supply Bills [for American Troops]—Proofs from the Record—The
Position of the Whig Party in Relation to the Mexican War—Ashmun's Res-
olution—Present Leaders of the Democracy [Nickname for the Democratic
Party] on the Mexican War—Slavery in the District of Columbia.

[Editor's Note: Even in "retirement," Mr. Lincoln, only 32 years old, as-
pired to higher office, e.g., U.S. congressman for his hometown of Springfield.
However, in the early 1840s, better-known rivals brushed him aside. There
was, though, a portent of better days. In 1844, his old idol of the Whig Party,
the moderate Henry Clay, age 67, finally won the presidential vote of the
Springfield district. The opposing and usually dominant Democratic Party
(nicknamed "the Democracy") momentarily retreated. In the next election,
with renewed inspiration, Mr. Lincoln jumped back into the political fray.]

In 1846, Mr. Lincoln received the unanimous nomination for
Congress by the Whig Convention for the Springfield district.
In 1844, the district had given a majority of 914 to Mr. Clay
[a winning margin of 7 percent of the total vote of 12,812]; and the
Democracy [aka the opposing Democrats] expected in the congressional election of 1846 to greatly lessen, if not entirely overcome,
this majority. With the hope of securing the latter result, they [the
Democrats] put in nomination [against Mr. Lincoln] Reverend Peter
Cartwright, the famous Methodist preacher[1]—a man of great popularity with the people generally, and especially popular with his
own denomination (which embraced a very large and influential
portion of the population of the district).

[In the congressional campaign of 1846] Mr. Lincoln spoke in
the principal towns in the district on the political issues of the day.
His opponent did not meet him in discussion [to debate], but chose
his own peculiar way of electioneering. [Rev. Cartwright hinted that
Mr. Lincoln was hostile to Christianity; Mr. Lincoln strongly denied

---

[1] Peter Cartwright (1785-1872) specialized in fire-and-brimstone sermons.

Library of Congress

"So Desperately in Love"
Matched daguerreotypes of Mary and Abraham Lincoln in 1846, the year of his election to Congress, and only four years after marriage. Mrs. Lincoln recalled they were so young and "so desperately in love."

it.] The canvass resulted in the election of Mr. Lincoln by a majority of 1,511 [a winning margin of 13 percent of 11,418 voters]—a majority unprecedented in the district, and conclusive as to the estimation in which he was held by his immediate neighbors.

Mr. Lincoln took his seat in the national House of Representatives [in Washington, D.C.,] on the seventh of December 1847—the beginning of the first session of the Thirtieth Congress. He met there such men as John Quincy Adams [Whig-Mass.,[1] former U.S. president, and son of the American Revolutionary John Adams]; George Ashmun [Whig-Mass., chairman of the Republican convention of 1860 that nominated Mr. Lincoln for president]; Jacob Collamer [Whig-Vt., future U.S. senator, and advocate of strong action against proslavery rebels during the Civil War]; John M. Botts [Whig-Va., conservative Southerner who denounced the rebellion, and remained loyal to the U.S. government]; Washington Hunt [Whig-N.Y., future neutralist governor of New York]; J.R. Ingersoll

---

[1] *[Whig-Mass.]* means *Whig from Massachusetts.* All are U.S. representatives.

[Whig-Pa., antislavery ally of Congressman Lincoln]; T. Butler King [Whig-Ga., future European emissary of the proslavery Confederate States]; Henry W. Hilliard [Whig-Ala., future Confederate general]; George P. Marsh [Whig-Vt., future ambassador to Italy for President Lincoln]; Charles S. Morehead [Whig-Ky., future governor of Kentucky, and Confederate sympathizer]; Meredith P. Gentry [Whig-Tenn., future congressman of the Confederacy who was captured and invalided home by President Lincoln]; James Pollock [Whig-Pa., housemate in Washington, future antislavery governor of Pennsylvania, and director of U.S. Mint for President Lincoln]; Caleb B. Smith [Whig-Ind., future secretary of the interior for President Lincoln]; Truman Smith [Whig-Conn., future U.S. senator, and President Lincoln's international representative for halting the overseas slave trade]; Robert C. Schenck [Whig-Ohio, future general in the U.S. Army]; Alexander H. Stephens [Whig-Ga., ally of Mr. Lincoln in

Robert Lincoln (1843-1926)
Eldest Son

He was only three years old when his father was elected to Congress in 1846. The son later attended Harvard; served as a U.S. Army officer in the Civil War; and lived to see the age of the automobile and airplane.

Library of Congress

U.S. Capitol, 1848
Congressman Lincoln lived in a nearby boarding house.

protesting the Mexican War, and future vice president of the Confederacy]; John B. Thompson [Whig-Ky., future U.S. senator], Robert Toombs [Whig-Ga., future secretary of state of the Confederacy], Samuel F. Vinton [Whig-Ohio, future antislavery assistant to President Lincoln], and other prominent Whig leaders. And although [Mr. Lincoln was then] a new man in Congress, and comparatively young, he at once took a prominent position among this brilliant array of distinguished men.

Throughout his congressional career, his record is that of a consistent Whig. On all the issues that divided parties which were brought before Congress for action, his name will be found recorded on the same side on which Clay and Webster had so often before recorded theirs.

[Editor's Note: Henry Clay (1777-1852) and Daniel Webster (1782-1852) were moderate, well-respected presidential contenders of the Whig Party. For decades, beginning in the 1830s, young Mr. Lincoln saw them as his role models and avidly agreed with their policies. Their joint platform included peaceful compromise on slavery; government spending for economic development; grants of public land for family farmers; and a tariff to protect U.S. workers and industries from unfair foreign competition. In the 1860 presidential contest, Mr. Lincoln adopted these policies as his own and presented himself as the faithful heir of Clay and Webster. (See New Appendix B.)]

Opposing a War, but Supporting the Troops

As a young congressman in 1847, Abraham Lincoln, along with many Northerners and moderate Southerners, denounced President James Polk's invasion and conquest of Mexico. Mr. Polk's allies retaliated by smearing Congressman Lincoln as a "Benedict Arnold" who failed to support American troops. The antiwar Mr. Lincoln retired at age 40, after only one term in Congress.

In 1860, a dozen years later, Mr. Lincoln still felt compelled to defend his antiwar stance. In his campaign biography, he offers "nuance"—he supported American troops, but opposed an unnecessary war and a disassembling president. (President Polk claimed that Mexico was the aggressor. Young Mr. Lincoln dared to doubt him.)

[The Mexican-American War]

A great deal has been said by his [Lincoln's] political opponents in regard to his action on the subject of the Mexican War; and in the canvass of 1858 with Mr. Douglas [during their race for the U.S. Senate], that gentleman and his newspaper organs made a very disingenuous, but characteristic attempt to fasten upon Mr. Lincoln a charge of having voted against supplies for the American Army in Mexico. The charge was without foundation in fact, and utterly untrue in every particular.

[Before Mr. Lincoln arrived in Washington in December 1847, General Winfield Scott, the commander of a U.S. amphibious invasion of Mexico, had already completed his conquest.][1] When Mr. Lincoln took his seat in Congress, General Scott had been nearly three months in possession of the City of Mexico [capital of the country]. All the great battles of that war had been fought, and the negotiations which resulted in the Treaty of Guadalupe Hidalgo on the second of February 1848, had progressed very far towards a favorable conclusion. The American Army, however, was still in Mexico; and various supply measures, resolutions of thanks, acts

---

[1] Winfield Scott (1786-1866) was still general-in-chief of the U.S. Army at age 75, when Mr. Lincoln assumed the presidency in March 1861.

The Conquest of Mexico
Contemporary lithograph depicts the bloody Battle of Cerro Gordo in 1847. It was the prelude to capturing Mexico City, the capital of the country.

for extra pay, and for the relief of the widows and orphans of officers and soldiers who had fallen in the war, were brought before the Thirtieth Congress [1847-49], and passed.

Mr. Lincoln voted in favor of every measure of this kind which came before Congress. A careful examination of the *Journals* and the *Congressional Globe*[1] discloses the fact that fourteen Acts and eight Joint Resolutions of the character referred to, were passed by this Congress. Of these, three Acts and two Joint Resolutions were passed under a call for the Ayes and Nays; the remainder without. We have the assurance of those who served in Congress with Mr. Lincoln—both his political friends and opponents—that he voted in favor of all the latter; while as to the former, the *House Journal* contains the proof.

The first of these Acts, which passed the House by Ayes and Nays, will be found in U.S. *Statutes at Large*, page 215, chapter 23, being "An Act further to supply deficiencies in the Appropriations for the Service of the Fiscal Year ending the thirtieth of June,

---

[1] The *House Journal* and the *Congressional Globe* were respectively records of votes and transcripts of debates in the U.S. Congress.

James K. Polk (1795-1849)
U.S. President, 1845-49

President Polk was a slaveholder from
Tennessee, and an ardent advocate of ex-
panding U.S. territory.

eighteen hundred and forty-eight"; and it appropriates, among other items, various sums distinctly for the benefit of volunteers in the
Mexican War, amounting to $7,508,939.74 *[about $175 million in*
modern dollars]. Mr. Lincoln's name is recorded in the affirmative.
(See *House Journal*, First Session, Thirtieth Congress, pages 520-21.)

The next Act, will be found in the *Statutes at Large*, page 217,
chapter 26, being "An Act to authorize a loan not to exceed the
sum of sixteen millions of dollars *[about $373 million in modern*
dollars]." This act was passed to provide money to meet appropriations in general, including those for the Mexican War, and would
not have been necessary but for that war. Mr. Lincoln's name stands
recorded in the affirmative. (See *House Journal*, pages 420-27.)

The last Act of this character passed by Ayes and Nays, will be
found in *Statutes at Large*, page 247, chap. 104, being "An Act to
amend an Act, entitled 'An Act supplemental to An Act entitled An
Act providing for the prosecution of the existing war between the
United States and the Republic of Mexico, and for other purposes.'" This Act, among other things, provided for giving three
months extra pay to officers, non-commissioned officers, musicians
and privates, engaged in the Mexican War, and to their relations, in
case of their dying in the service. Mr. Lincoln's name is recorded in
favor of this Act. (See *House Journal*, page 768.)

The two Joint Resolutions spoken of will be found in *Statutes at*
Large, pages 333 and 334. They were expressive of the thanks of

Mr. Lincoln's First Political Party: The Whigs

Abraham Lincoln entered the Thirtieth Congress (1847-49) as a member of the now extinct Whigs. Their political party was unified

North and South by a platform of economic development, or "internal improvements." The Whigs admired George Washington and John Adams as Founding Fathers of honor and principle. Both Northern and Southern Whigs opposed the invasion of Mexico in 1846-48.

However, the dispute over slavery would gradually split them. Antislavery Whigs included

John Adams

the young Mr. Lincoln and John Quincy Adams, the 80-year-old son of John Adams. On the proslavery side were Alexander Stephens and Robert Toombs, respectively the future vice president and secretary of state of the Confederacy.

Many congressional Whigs later wistfully recalled their younger days. However, most grimly prosecuted a ghastly Civil War against each other. Sentiment could do little to ease their remorseless struggle over slavery.

John Quincy Adams

Congress to Major General Winfield Scott [who led a U.S. seaborne assault at Veracruz, Mexico] and Major General Zachary Taylor [who conducted a simultaneous land invasion from Texas], and to the troops under their command respectively, for their distinguished gallantry and good conduct in the Mexican campaign of 1847. Mr. Lincoln's name is recorded in favor of both resolutions. (See *House Journal*, pages [361-62], 365-66.)

These are the only instances that occurred while Mr. Lincoln was in Congress in which supplies, extra pay, or thanks were voted or proposed, under a call of the Ayes and Nays, for the American Army in Mexico; and in each case he is recorded in the affirmative.

Mr. Lincoln held, in common with the entire Whig Party of that day, that the war with Mexico was unnecessarily and unconstitutionally begun; and all who desire to know the reasons on which the Whig Party based this opinion, will find them most ably set forth in a speech delivered in Congress by Mr. Lincoln, January 12, 1848; and which may be found in the Appendix to the *Congressional Globe*, First Session, Thirtieth Congress, beginning at page 93.

Previous to the delivery of that speech, Mr. Lincoln had intentionally refrained from taking exceptions publicly to what he honestly believed to be the unjustifiable conduct of President Polk[1] in precipitating the country into a war with Mexico. The following extract from the speech contains the reasons which, in his [Lincoln's] judgment, demanded a departure from this line of policy:

[Mr. Lincoln Supports Troops, Not President Polk]

"When the war began, it was my opinion that all those who, because of knowing too *little*, or because of knowing too *much*, could not conscientiously approve the conduct of the President in the beginning of it, should, nevertheless, as good citizens and patriots, remain silent on that point, at least till the war should be ended. Some leading Democrats [who disagree with their party's president, Mr. Polk, on the Mexican War], including ex-President Van Buren,[2] have taken this same view, as I understand them; and I adhered to it, and acted upon it, until since I took my seat here, and I think I should still adhere to it, were it not that the President and his friends will not allow it to be so.

"Besides the continual effort of the President to argue every silent vote given for supplies into an endorsement[3] of the justice and wisdom of his conduct [in making war on Mexico]; besides that singularly candid paragraph in his late message, in

---

[1] James K. Polk (1795-1849), D-Tenn., U.S. president, 1845-49.

[2] Martin Van Buren (1782-1862), D-N.Y., U.S. president, 1837-41. He also ran for president in 1848 as the nominee of the antislavery Free Soil Party.

[3] *Endorse* replaces the archaic *indorse* in the original text.

Tarbell, 1907

Congressman-elect Lincoln, 1846

In private, friends noted an endearing gentleness, at odds with an increasingly heated public persona.

which he tells us that Congress, with great unanimity (only two in the Senate and fourteen in the House dissenting) had declared that 'by the act of the Republic of Mexico a state of war exists between that Government and the United States,' when the same journals that informed him of this, also informed him that, when that declaration stood disconnected from the question of supplies [for American troops], sixty-seven in the House [or nearly a third of all congressmen], and not fourteen merely, voted against it; besides this open attempt to prove by telling the *[partial] truth*, what he could not prove by telling the *whole truth*—demanding of all who will not submit to be misrepresented, in justice to themselves, to speak out; besides all this, one of my colleagues *[Mr. Richardson]*,[1] at a very early day in the session, brought in a set of resolutions, expressly endorsing the original justice of the war on the part of the President. Upon these resolutions, when they shall be put on their passage, I shall be *compelled* to vote [against]; so that I cannot be silent if I would."

As before observed, Mr. Lincoln did not stand alone in holding these views. They were held substantially by the entire Whig Party, both at the North and the South; as well as by Mr. Calhoun and those Southern men who at that time had adopted his peculiar political opinions. [Editor's Note: U.S. Senator John C. Calhoun, D-S.C., was a prominent ideologue and defender of slavery. He advocated "States' Rights" and the nullification by States of federal laws they disliked, e.g., restrictions on slavery. The Whig Party disagreed with him on these matters, but Mr. Calhoun still joined their opposition to the Mexican War.][2]

The following, from the *House Journal*, First Session, Thirtieth Congress, pages 183-84 (January 3, 1848), shows the position of the Whig Party on the subject [the Mexican War]:

---

[1]   Annotation from 1860 text; refers to U.S. Rep. William A. Richardson, D-Ill.

[2]   Senator John C. Calhoun (1782-1850) of South Carolina was a different person than John Calhoun (1806-59) of Illinois, a surveyor and mentor of young Mr. Lincoln in the 1830s. Both Calhouns, though, were proslavery. Mr. Lincoln often sought common ground with people of differing views.

The Southern Friend

Congressman Alexander Stephens (1812-83), a slaveholder from Georgia, also opposed the Mexican War. He gave conservative cover to the antiwar Mr. Lincoln. Yet Mr. Stephens later became vice president of the Confederacy that waged war against the United States and his old friend, then President Lincoln.

[House of Representatives Censures President Polk]

"In pursuance of previous notice, Mr. John W. Houston [D-Del.][1] asked, and obtained leave [or permission to speak], and introduced a joint resolution of thanks to Major-General Taylor [a commander of U.S. forces invading Mexico] and which was read a first and second time; when Mr. Schenck [Whig-Ohio] moved that the said resolution be referred to the Committee on Military Affairs, Mr. Henly [Thomas J. *Henley*, D-Ind.] moved to amend the said mot[ion] of Mr. Schenck by adding thereto the following: With instructions to insert in the said resolution the following: *'Engaged as they were, in defending the rights and honor of the country.'*

"Mr. Ashmun [Whig-Mass.] moved to amend the said proposed instructions by adding at the end of the same: *'In a war*

---

[1]   Party identifier *[D-Del.]*, or *Democrat from Delaware.*

unnecessarily and unconstitutionally begun by the President of the United States.'

"And the question was put, 'Will the House agree to the amendment offered by Mr. Ashmun?'

"And decided in the affirmative—Yeas 82; Nays 81.

"The yeas and nays being desired by one-fifth of the members present.

"Those who voted in the affirmative are—

"Mr. John Quincy Adams [Whig-Mass.], George Ashmun [Whig-Mass.], Daniel M. Barringer [Whig-N.C.], Washington Barrow [Whig-Tenn.], Hiram Belcher [Whig-Maine], John M. Botts [Whig-Va.], Jasper E. Brady [Whig-Pa.], Aylett Buckner [Whig-Ky.], Richard S. Canby [Whig-Ohio], Thomas L. Clingman [Whig-N.C.], William M. Cocke [Whig-Tenn.], Jacob Collamer [Whig-Vt.], Harmon S. Conger [Whig-N.Y.], Robert B. Cranston [Whig-R.I.], John Crowell [Whig-Ohio], John H. Crozier [Whig-Tenn.], John Dickey [Whig-Pa.], James Dixon [Whig-Conn.], Richard S. Donnell [Whig-N.C.], William Duer [Whig-N.Y.], Daniel Duncan [Whig-Ohio], Garnett Duncan [Whig-Ky.], George G. Dunn [Whig-Ind.], George N. Eckert [Whig-Pa.], Thomas O. Edwards [Whig-Ohio], Alexander Evans [Whig-Md.], Nathan Evans [Whig-Ohio], David Fisher [Whig-Ohio], Andrew S. Fulton [Whig-Va.], John Gayle [Whig-Ala.], Meredith P. Gentry [Whig-Tenn.], Joshua R. Giddings [Whig-Ohio], William L. Goggin [Whig-Va.]; Joseph Grinnell, Artemas Hale [Whigs-Mass]; Nathan K. Hall [Whig-N.Y.], James G. Hampton [Whig-N.J.], William T. Haskell [Whig-Tenn.], William Henry [Whig-Vt.], John W. Houston [Whig-Del.], Samuel D. Hubbard [Whig-Conn.], Charles Hudson [Whig-Mass.], Alexander Irvin [Whig-Pa.], Orlando Kellogg [Whig-N.Y.], T. Butler King [Whig-Ga.], Daniel P. King [Whig-Mass.], Abraham Lincoln [Whig-Ill.], Abraham K. McIlvane [Whig-Pa.], George P. Marsh [Whig-Vt.], Dudley Marvin [Whig-N.Y.], Joseph Mullin [Whig-N.Y.], Henry Nes [Whig-Pa.], William A. Newell [Whig-N.J.], William B. Preston [Whig-Va.], Harvey Putnam [Whig-N.Y.], Gideon Reynolds [Whig-N.Y.], Julius Rockwell [Whig-Mass.], John A. Rockwell [Whig-Conn.], Joseph M. Root [Whig-Ohio], David Rumsey Jr. [Whig-N.Y.], Daniel B. St. John [Whig-N.Y.], Robert C. Schenck [Whig-Ohio], Augustine H. Shepperd [Whig-N.C.], Eliakim Sherrill [Whig-N.Y.], John I. Slingerland [Whig-N.Y.], Caleb B. Smith [Whig-Ind.], Truman Smith [Whig-Conn.], Alexander H. Stephens [Whig-Ga.], Andrew Stewart [Whig-Pa.], John Strohm [Whig-Pa.], Peter H. Sylvester [Peter H. *Silvester*, Whig-N.Y.], Bannon G. Thibodeaux [Whig-La.], John L. Taylor [Whig-Ohio], Patrick W. Tompkins [Whig-Miss.], Richard W. Thompson [Whig-Ind.], John B. Thompson [Whig-Ky.], Robert Toombs [Whig-Ga.], Amos Tuck [Ind-N.H.],[1] John Van Dyke [Whig-N.J.], Samuel F. Vinton [Whig-Ohio], Cornelius Warren [Whig-N.Y.], James Wilson [Whig-N.H.]."

It will be seen, by inspection of the foregoing names, that some of the most distinguished leaders of the Democracy of the present day voted with Mr. Lincoln [to censure President Polk and his war.]

[Editor's Note: In the 1860 presidential campaign, the "Democracy," i.e., the Democrats of rival Stephen Douglas, questioned Mr. Lincoln's patriotism for opposing the Mexican War. The above passage replies that some conservative Democrats, including proslavery Southerners, were also antiwar. They cannot credibly denounce Mr. Lincoln in 1860 if they agreed with him then.

However, annotating the above roster suggests that the text here mistakingly refers to a *different* resolution of 1846. (See page 101.) In the above tally of 1848, all but one of the antiwar votes are from Mr. Lincoln's own Whig Party. They unite in a partisan rebuke of Democratic President James Polk and his invasion of Mexico. Years later, as slavery became a bigger issue, some antiwar Whigs of the South switched to the proslavery Democrats, but long after the Mexican War ended. In 1848, with U.S. troops still in Mexico, most old-line Democrats deferred to their party's controversial leader, President Polk.]

It will also be seen that, while the resolution censured the President for the manner in which he began the war, it also conveyed the thanks of Congress to the officers and soldiers of the American army, for their gallant defense of the rights and honor of the country.

Mr. Lincoln's reasons for the opinion expressed by this vote, as subsequently stated in his speech on the war, were, briefly, that the President had sent General Taylor into an inhabited part of the

---

[1] *Ind.*, or *Independent*, i.e., not affiliated with a political party.

country belonging to Mexico, and thereby had provoked the first act of hostility; that the place at which these hostilities were provoked, being the country bordering on the east bank of the Rio Grande [a river flowing between Texas and Mexico], was inhabited by native Mexicans born there under the Mexican government, and had never submitted to, nor been conquered by Texas or the United States, nor transferred to either by treaty; that although Texas claimed the Rio Grande as her boundary, Mexico had never recognized it, the people on the ground had never recognized it, and neither Texas nor the United States had ever enforced it; that there was a broad desert between that [claimed] and the country over which Texas had actual control; [and] that the country where hostilities commenced, having once belonged to Mexico, must remain so until it was somehow legally transferred, which had never been done.

Mr. Lincoln thought the act of sending an armed force among the Mexicans was *unnecessary* inasmuch as Mexico was in no way molesting or menacing the United States or the people thereof; and that it was *unconstitutional*, because the power of levying war was vested in Congress, and not in the President. He thought the prin-

Zachary Taylor (1784-1850)
General, U.S. Army, 1837-48

President Polk ordered him to invade Mexico. This 1847 print suggests inner doubts. General Taylor was a Whig like young Mr. Lincoln.

Library of Congress

cipal motive for the act was to divert public attention from the surrender by the Democratic Party [led by President Polk] of "Fifty-four forty, or fight,"[1] to Great Britain on the Oregon boundary question. [President Polk never fulfilled his campaign promise to enlarge Oregon Territory at the expense of British-ruled Canada.]

He [Lincoln] also doubtless believed that it [the invasion of Mexico] was an intentional bid of the Democratic Party for Southern support, inasmuch as the conquest of all or any portion of Mexico would be hailed by the South as an assurance of the extension of slavery, and an increase of the political power, in the federal government, of the slaveholding interest.

The adoption of Ashmun's amendment [sponsored by U.S. Rep. George Ashmun, Whig-Mass.] was not the first occasion the Whig Party, through its representatives in Congress, had condemned the act of the President in involving the country in a war with Mexico. On the eleventh of May 1846, as will be seen by reference to the *House Journal*, pp. 792-93, the following action was had:

> "On motion to amend a bill for an act providing for the prosecution of the existing war between the United States and the Republic of Mexico, by inserting the following preamble:
>
> "'Whereas, by the act of the Republic of Mexico, a state of war exists between that government and the United States—'
>
> "It was decided in the affirmative—yeas 123, noes 67."

[Those voting "no" rejected President Polk's claim that Mexico started the war.] The Northern Whigs voted solidly in the negative, as well as the following Southern members:

> "Daniel M. Barringer ([Whig]-N.C.), Thomas H. Bayly ([D]-Va.), Henry Bedinger ([D]-Va.), Armisted Burt ([D]-S.C.), John H. Crozier ([Whig]-Tenn.), Garrett Davis ([Whig]-Ky.), Alfred Dockery ([Whig]-N.C.), Henry Grider ([Whig]-Ky.), Henry W. Hilliard ([Whig]-Ala.), Isaac E. Holmes ([D]-S.C.), John W. Hous-

---

[1] The U.S. then claimed British Columbia as far north as 54° 40' North latitude. The modern boundary is at 49° North, considerably to the South.

ton ([Whig]-Del.), Edmund W. Hubard ([D]-Va.), Robert T. M. Hunter ([D]-Va.), T. Butler King ([Whig]-Ga.), John H. McHenry ([Whig]-Ky.), John S. Pendleton ([Whig]-Va.), R. Barnwell Rhett ([D]-S.C.), James A. S[edd]on ([D]-Va.), Alexander D. Sims ([D]-S.C.), Richard F. Simpson ([D]-S.C.), Alexander H. Stephens ([Whig]-Ga.), Robert Toombs ([Whig]-Ga.), Joseph A. Woodward ([D]-S.C.), William L. Yancey ([D]-Ala.)."

It will be seen that the above list includes a number of the most prominent of the leaders of modern Democracy [aka the Democratic Party of President Polk and Stephen Douglas]. Like Mr. Lincoln, they believed the war to have been "unnecessarily and unconstitutionally begun"; but like him, they also discriminated between the honor of the country and the gallant services of the American troops on the one hand, and the act of the President on the other. This point was brought out very clearly by Mr. Lincoln in a speech delivered in the House of Representatives, July 27, 1848, of which the following is an extract:

[Mr. Lincoln Praises Bipartisan Heroism]

"The declaration that we have always opposed the war is true or false, accordingly as we may understand the term, 'opposing the war.' If to say, 'the war was unnecessarily and unconstitutionally commenced by the President,' be opposing the war, then the Whigs have very generally opposed it. Whenever they have spoken at all, they have said this, and they have said it on what has appeared good reason to them. The marching [of] an army into the midst of a peaceful Mexican settlement— frightening the inhabitants away, leaving their growing crops and other property to destruction—to *you* may appear a perfectly amiable, peaceful, unprovoking procedure, but it does not appear so to *us*. So to call such an act, to us appears no other than a naked, impudent absurdity, and we speak of it accordingly.

"But if, when the war had begun, and had become the cause of the country, the giving of our money and our blood, in com-

Death of a Soldier, 1847
Henry Clay, Jr., fell in battle in Mexico, traumatizing the nation. He was the son of Henry Clay, Sr., the respected leader of Mr. Lincoln's antiwar party, the Whigs. The senior Mr. Clay lost the previous presidential election; but for that loss, a war with Mexico might never have occurred.

mon with yours, was support of the war, then it is not true that we have always opposed the war. With few individual exceptions, you have constantly had our votes here for all the necessary supplies. And more than this, you have had the services, the blood, and the lives of our political brethren in every trial, and on every field. The beardless boy and the mature man—the humble and the distinguished—you have had them. Through suffering and death—by disease and in battle—they have endured, and fought, and fallen with you.

"Clay and Webster each gave a son [in Mexico], never to be returned.[1] From the State of my own residence, besides other worthy but less-known Whig names, we sent Marshall, Morrison, Baker, and Hardin—they all fought, and one fell; and in

---

[1]   Henry Clay and Daniel Webster were leaders of the antiwar Whig Party.

the fall of that one we lost our best Whig man [Colonel John J. Hardin].[1] Nor were the Whigs few in number, or laggard in the day of danger. In that fearful, bloody, breathless struggle at Buena Vista [near Monterrey, Mexico, in 1847], where each man's hard task was to beat back five foes, or die himself, of the five high officers who perished, four were Whigs.

Battle of Buena Vista, 1847

"In speaking of this, I mean no odious comparison between the lion-hearted Whigs and Democrats who fought there. On other occasions, and among the lower officers and privates on *that* occasion, I doubt not the proportion was different. I wish to do justice to all. I think of all those brave men as Americans, in whose proud fame, as an American, I too have a share. Many of them, Whigs and Democrats, are my constituents and personal friends; and I thank them—more than thank them— one and all, for the high, imperishable honor they have con- ferred on our common State [Illinois].

"But the distinction between the cause of the *President* in be- ginning the war, and the cause of the *country* after it was be- gun, is a distinction which you can not perceive. To *you* the President and the country seem to be all one. You are interest-

---

[1]   John J. Hardin (1810-47) formerly held Mr. Lincoln's seat in Congress.

ed to see no distinction between them, and I venture to suggest that *possibly* your interest blinds you a little.

"We see the distinction, as we think, clearly enough; and our friends who have fought in the war have no difficulty in seeing it also. What those who have fallen would say, were they alive and here, of course, we can never know; but with those who have returned, there is no difficulty. Colonel Haskell and Major Gaines, members here,[1] both fought in the war, and one of them underwent extraordinary perils and hardships; still they, like all other Whigs here, vote on the record that the war was unnecessarily and unconstitutionally commenced by the President.

And even General Taylor himself, the noblest Roman[2] of them all [and also a Whig], has declared that as a citizen, and particularly as a soldier, it is sufficient for him to know that his country is at war with a foreign nation, to do all in his power to bring it to a speedy and honorable termination by the most vigorous and energetic operations, without inquiring about its justice, or anything else connected with it."

[Editor's Note: Mr. Lincoln's antiwar activities were unpopular in his congressional district, ending his first political career. However, by speaking his mind, he returned to boyhood ideals—George Washington's virtue. Mr. Lincoln never again sought popularity for its own sake. (He once claimed 98 percent of the vote in his hometown.) Nevertheless, a decade without political office followed, due in no small part to a new outspokenness.]

The Thirtieth Congress [1847-49] was made famous by the introduction and discussion of the Wilmot Proviso[3] [a failed proposal to ban slavery from lands captured from Mexico, including California and the American Southwest]. Mr. Lincoln supported this measure from first to last, being then as now, uncompromisingly opposed to the extension of slavery into free territory. He is also on record in favor of the improvement of rivers and harbors, and the appropriation of public lands in aid of great and important public improvements.

---

[1] U.S. Reps. William T. Haskell, Whig-Tenn., and John P. Gaines, Whig-Ky.

[2] Romans were supposedly the epitome of martial and republican values.

[3] Sponsored by U.S. Rep. David Wilmot (1814-68), D-Pa.

[Early Views on Slavery]

[Editor's Note: In the 1860 presidential campaign, Abraham Lincoln advocated barring slavery from new Territories of the American West.[1] However, Mr. Lincoln opposed ending slavery in existing States, e.g., the Deep South. Some thought him posturing, being all things to all people.

In reality, these were his views for decades. He only wanted to halt slavery's growth, prohibiting new slavery on new lands. Existing slavery, he believed, would decline naturally due to modernization of the economy. Mr. Lincoln predicted slaveholders would someday voluntarily free slaves.

His views were then common in the moderate Whig Party, but many viewed them skeptically. Mr. Lincoln's below proposal to free slaves in Washington, D.C., illustrates the point. Despite his bill's complexity, nothing happens if voters, i.e., slaveholders, object to freeing slaves. Both pro- and antislavery congressmen disliked Mr. Lincoln's plan, and he withdrew it.]

[Abolition of Slavery, Washington, D. C.]

The subject of slavery in the District of Columbia was also before the Thirtieth Congress. Mr. Lincoln prepared and submitted a bill embodying his views on that subject, which is here presented to the reader. The bill is entitled, "A bill to abolish Slavery in the District of Columbia, by consent of the free white people of said District, and with compensation to owners," and may be found in the *Congressional Globe*, vol. 20, page 212, as follows:

"Section 1. *Be it enacted by the Senate and House of Representatives of the United States in Congress assembled,* That no person not now within the District of Columbia nor now owned by any person or persons now resident within it, nor hereafter born within it, shall ever be held in slavery within said District.

"§ 2. That no person now within said District, or now owned by any person or persons now resident within the same, or hereafter born within it, shall ever be held in slavery without [or outside] the limits of said District: *Provided,* That officers of the Government of the United States, being citizens of the slaveholding States, coming into said District on public business, and remaining only so long as may be reasonably necessary for that object, may be attended into and out of said

---

[1] *Territories* were precursors of States, but had no votes in national elections.

Antislavery Poster
New York City, 1837

Young Mr. Lincoln deemed slavery wrong, but rejected impassioned appeals (right) to immediately abolish it. He feared violence from owners.

Library of Congress

District, and while there, by the necessary servants of themselves and their families, without their right to hold such servants in service being thereby impaired.[1]

"§ 3. That all children born of slave mothers, within said District, on or after the first day of January, in the year of our Lord one thousand eight hundred and fifty [1850], shall be free; but shall be reasonably supported and educated by the respective owners of their mothers, or by their heirs or representatives, and shall owe reasonable service, as apprentices, to such owners, heirs and representatives, until they respectively arrive at the age of —— years,[2] when they shall be entirely free. And the municipal authorities of Washington and Georgetown [an adjacent settlement], within their respective jurisdictional limits, are hereby empowered and required to make all suitable and necessary provisions for enforcing obedience to this section, on the part of both masters and apprentices.

[1] E.g., presidents and congressmen who have slaves can keep them.
[2] Mr. Lincoln intended to later determine an age of maturity.

Street Sale of Slaves, 1861
Engraving depicts auction of black slaves (on stage).

"§ 4. That all persons now within said District lawfully held as slaves, or now owned by any person or persons now resident within said District, shall remain such at the will of their respective owners, their heirs and legal representatives: *Provided*, That any such owner, or his legal representatives, may at any time receive from the Treasury of the United States the full value of his or her slave of the class in this section mentioned; upon which such slave shall be forthwith and forever free: *And provided further*, That the President of the United States, the Secretary of State, and the Secretary of the Treasury, shall be a board for determining the value of such slaves as their owners may desire to emancipate under this section, and whose duty it shall be to hold a session for the purpose on the first Monday of each calendar month; to receive all applications, and, on satisfactory evidence in each case that the person presented for valuation is a slave, and of the class in this section mentioned, and is owned by the applicant, shall value such slave at his or her full cash value, and give to the applicant an order on the treasury for the amount, and also to such slaves a certificate of freedom.

"§ 5. That the municipal authorities of Washington and Georgetown, within their respective jurisdictional limits, are hereby empowered and required to provide active and efficient means to arrest and deliver up to their owners all fugitive slaves escaping into said District.

"§ 6. That the election officers within said District of Columbia are hereby empowered and required to open polls at all the usual places of holding elections on the first Monday of April next, and receive the vote of every free white male citizen above the age of twenty-one years, having resided within said District for the period of one year or more next preceding the time of such voting for or against this act, to proceed in taking said votes in all respects not herein specified, as at elections under the municipal laws, and with as little delay as possible to transmit correct statements of the votes so cast, to the President of the United States; and it shall be the duty of the President to canvass said votes immediately, and if a majority of them be found to be for this act, to forthwith issue his proclamation giving notice of the fact; and this act shall only be in full force and effect on and after the day of such proclamation.

"§ 7. That involuntary servitude for the punishment of crime whereof the party shall have been duly convicted, shall in nowise be prohibited by this act.

"§ 8. That for all the purposes of this act, the jurisdictional limits of Washington are extended to all parts of the District of Columbia not now included within the present limits of Georgetown."

In submitting this proposition, Mr. Lincoln stated that it had the approval of a number of the leading citizens of the District. Among them, it is understood, were Messrs. Gales and Seaton of the *National Intelligencer*, the latter of whom was then Mayor of the City of Washington. [Joseph Gales and William Seaton were conservative publishers of the city's major newspaper.]

These views were not new with Mr. Lincoln. As early as in 1837, while a member of the state legislature, he had given them expression in the following protest which was entered on the *House Journal*:

"March 3, 1837

"The following protest was presented to the House [the lower chamber of the General Assembly, or State Legislature of Illinois], which was read and ordered to be spread on the journals, to wit:

"Resolutions upon the subject of domestic slavery having passed both branches of the General Assembly at its present session, the undersigned hereby protest against the passage of the same. [The resolutions praised slavery and condemned abolitionists, those seeking Federal action to immediately end slavery.]

"They believe that the institution of slavery is founded on both injustice and bad policy; but that the promulgation of abolition doctrines tends rather to increase than abate its evils.

"They believe that the Congress of the United States has no power, under the Constitution, to interfere with the institution of slavery in the different States.

"They believe that the Congress of the United States has the power, under the Constitution, to abolish slavery in the District of Columbia; but that *that*[1] power ought not to be exercised unless at the request of the people of said District.

"The difference between these opinions and those contained in the said resolutions, is their reason for entering this protest.

DAN STONE, A. LINCOLN,[2]
Representatives from the County of Sangamon [Illinois]."

That his opinions on this subject have undergone no change is evident from his reply to an interrogatory of Mr. [Stephen] Douglas at the Freeport debate [during their contest for the U.S. Senate] in 1858, as to whether he (Lincoln) did not stand pledged to the abolition of slavery in the District of Columbia. Mr. Lincoln said he was not so pledged, and added:

---

[1] Emphasis added to the second *that* in the phrase *that that.*

[2] Mr. Lincoln's mild protest against slavery weakened him politically. After squeaking through reelection in 1840, he retired from the legislature at age 32.

"Contraband," 1862
Even after the Civil War began in 1861, President Lincoln honored his biography's promise not *to forcibly free slaves. He initially deemed confiscated slaves of opposing rebel troops as "contraband," not liberated peoples.*

[The Foul Blot]

"In relation to that, I have my mind very distinctly made up. I should be exceedingly glad to see slavery abolished in the District of Columbia. I believe that Congress possesses the constitutional power to abolish it. Yet, as a member of Congress, I should not, with my present views, be in favor of endeavoring to abolish slavery in the District of Columbia, unless it would be upon these conditions: First, that the abolition should be gradual; second, that it should be on a vote of the majority of qualified voters in the District; and third, that compensation should be made to unwilling owners. With these three conditions, I confess I would be exceedingly glad to see Congress abolish slavery in the District of Columbia, and in the language of Henry Clay, 'sweep from our capital that foul blot upon our nation.'"

Chapter Eight [Seven]¹
[Retirement to Springfield]

Reason for Retiring from Congress—The Canvass of 1852—Repeal of the
Missouri Compromise—Again in Politics—Encounters with Douglas—Re-
treat of the "Little Giant"—An Opposition Legislature—Election of U.S.
Senator—Magnanimous Conduct of Mr. Lincoln—Organization of the Republican Party in Illinois—Speech of 1857.

Mr. Lincoln was not a candidate for reelection to Congress [in 1848]. This was determined upon and publicly declared before he went to Washington, in accordance with an understanding among leading Whigs of the district,
and by virtue of which Colonel John J. Hardin and Colonel E. D.
Baker [Mr. Lincoln's predecessors in Congress] had each previously
served a single term from the same district.²

[In the presidential contest of 1848, the Whigs nominated General Zachary Taylor, a hero of the Mexican War. Congress adjourned
in August, and Mr. Lincoln campaigned for him.] After the adjournment he spoke several times by invitation, in advocacy of the election of General Taylor, both in Maryland and Massachusetts; and
on his [Lincoln's] return to Illinois, he canvassed his own district
very thoroughly, which was followed by a majority in the district of
over 1,500 for the Whig electoral ticket. [This was a winning margin
for General Taylor of 11 percent of the 13,253 voters in the Springfield district. The war hero also won nationally, becoming president.]

After the presidential election of 1848, Mr. Lincoln applied himself more closely than ever to the practice of his profession [as a
lawyer]. In 1852 [the next presidential election], he was again
placed by his Whig friends upon the Scott electoral ticket, but his
professional engagements, together with the utter hopelessness of

---

¹ The 1860 text skips from Chapter Six to Chapter Eight. This may be a typo-
graphic error, but publishers also shortened the book to save costs.
² Reelection was also impractical. Mr. Lincoln's opposition to the Mexican
War made him unpopular with many voters. Mr. Scripps minimizes this by
noting that Mr. Lincoln was still in demand as a speaker.

Zachary Taylor (1784-1850)
U.S. President, 1849-50

He opposed more land for slavery, but died after only sixteen months as president. Image is from an 1848 poster.

Library of Congress

the cause in Illinois, deterred him from making as active and thorough a canvass of the State as he had done on former like occasions. [Mr. Lincoln was pledged in the Electoral College for General Winfield Scott, another war hero running for president.] [1]

[Thereafter, Mr. Lincoln focused on his law practice.] In 1854, his profession had almost superseded all thought of politics. He had abandoned all political aspirations, content, as it seemed, with the honors which his profession brought him. The country was once more free from excitement. The agitation which grew out of the acquisition of territory from Mexico had been quieted by the compromise measures of 1850. [Congress shared captured Mexican territory between anti- and proslavery partisans. California became a Free State; the remaining lands had the option of slavery.] Each of the political parties had expressed a determination in national convention to abide by that settlement of the slavery question.

[Kansas-Nebraska Roils America, 1854]

[Hence, from 1850 to 1854, slavery was not a major issue for most people.] The status of all our unsettled territory [in the American West] was now fixed by law, so far as this subject was concerned. Sectional jealousies were obliterated, sectional strife healed,

---

[1]   General Winfield Scott, a moderate Whig, lost the 1852 presidential election to Franklin Pierce (1804-69), a Democrat allied with slaveholders.

and concord and repose marked our enviable condition. From this peaceful and happy state, the country was suddenly and unexpectedly aroused [in 1854], as "by the sound of a firebell at night,"[1] by the introduction of a bill [the Kansas-Nebraska Act] into the United States Senate for the repeal of the Missouri Compromise. [The compromise had peacefully divided prewar America into pro- and antislavery regions, especially its frontier Territories of the West.]

What followed is painfully fresh in the public recollection. The country was convulsed as it never had been before, and wise men clearly foresaw the evils that have since come upon us—and from which we have not yet recovered.

[Editor's Note: Mr. Lincoln's old rival, U.S. Senator Stephen Douglas, D-Ill., sponsored the Kansas-Nebraska Act of 1854. The law ended the last peaceful compromise on slavery. Guerrilla war soon erupted in Kansas, then a new Territory of the West. Local partisans battled, killing hundreds.

The strategic dynamic was also one-sided. Congress previously reserved Kansas for a free society. A struggle there might create more slavery, but not less. Also vulnerable were the future Nebraska, Dakotas, Montana, Wyoming, and Colorado—all covered by the Kansas-Nebraska Act.]

[Mr. Lincoln's Protest]

[The Missouri Compromise had kept the peace on slavery since 1820, or more than three decades.] The repeal of this time-honored compact aroused Mr. Lincoln as he never had been before. He at once perceived the conflicts that must grow out of it; the angry strife between the North and the South, and the struggles in Kansas. He saw in the Kansas-Nebraska bill [or the Nebraska bill for short] a wide departure from the mode pursued by the [Founding] Fathers of dealing with slavery—that while the policy of the latter was based upon a recognition of its wrongfulness, the Nebraska bill proceeded upon the opposite hypothesis, that it is not wrong.

He [Lincoln] saw and he foretold—before the Supreme Court had decided the *Dred Scott* case [overturning all bans on slavery in the new Territories of the West]—that the judiciary would not be slow to endorse the doctrine of Congress and the President; and that thus, each of the coordinate branches of the federal govern-

---

[1] Paraphrase of Thomas Jefferson in 1820, warning of conflict over slavery.

ment would stand committed against the early belief that slavery is wrong, as well as against the early policy based upon that belief.

Not only did he [Lincoln] regard the Nebraska bill, therefore, as inaugurating a complete revolution in the policy of the government, but as artfully designed to lay the foundation for a revolution in the moral sentiment of the country, preparatory to the establishment of slavery in the Free States, as well as in the Territories [of the American West], and the revival of the African slave trade.[1]

[Democrats Split Over Slavery]

On his [Douglas's] return to Illinois [from Washington, D.C., in August 1854] after the passage of his Kansas-Nebraska bill, Mr. Douglas saw the mischief which that measure had wrought in the ranks of his party in his own State, and forthwith undertook to repair it. [Fellow Democrats objected to his Kansas-Nebraska Act, believing it favored slave States, and harmed Illinois, where slavery was banned.]

A legislature was to be elected in November of that year, on which would devolve the duty of electing a successor to General Shields [Illinois's other senator] in the U.S. Senate.[2] It was a matter of great importance to Mr. Douglas to secure the reelection of General Shields [a Senate ally on the Kansas-Nebraska Act], as his defeat would be tantamount to a censure upon himself. He [Douglas] commenced his labors in Chicago, where he met with anything but a flattering reception from a con-

Stephen Douglas, Circa 1855

---

[1] In 1808, Congress banned new imports of slaves from Africa, hoping existing slavery would then decline. Smuggling, though, continued. By the 1850s, slaveholders sought to formally end the ban, seeking new slaves for expansion.

[2] U.S. Senator James Shields (1810-79), D-Ill., earned the title "General" from military service in the Mexican War, 1846-48.

Harper's Weekly 1863/Library of Congress

Bleeding Kansas, 1854-65

The Civil War began early in frontier Kansas and lasted a decade. Proslavery guerrillas twice raided the town of Lawrence, in 1856 and 1863 (above).

stituency whom he had deceived, and whose moral sense he had grossly outraged. **[Editor's Note: Many now saw Senator Douglas as a friend of slavery. In Chicago, angry protesters burned him in effigy. Some blamed his well-known ambition to be president: He allegedly betrayed Illinois and other Free States to win support from slaveholders of the South.]**[1]

Thence he went to Springfield, the capital of the State. He arrived there at the time the State Agricultural Society was holding its annual fair [in early October 1854]. The occasion had brought together a vast multitude of people from all parts of the State. Hundreds of politicians had also assembled, among whom were many of the ablest men of the State. [Mr. Lincoln, a resident of Springfield, went to the fair after learning of Mr. Douglas's presence.] Much time was devoted to political speaking, but the great event of the occasion was the debate between Lincoln and Douglas.

[Impromptu Debate, Lincoln & Douglas, 1854]

It had been nearly fourteen years since these gentlemen had been pitted against each other in a public discussion. In the canvass of 1840, Lincoln had proved himself more than a match for Douglas in debate [arguing for their respective presidential nomi-

---

[1]   In September 1854, Frederick Douglass, the antislavery activist, also came to Chicago to lambaste "degeneracy," Stephen Douglas, and the Kansas-Nebraska Act. The ex-slave, though, first met Mr. Lincoln in 1863 during the Civil War.

nees of the Whig and Democratic Parties]. But during most of the intervening years, the latter [Douglas] had occupied a position either in the national House of Representatives, or in the United States Senate, where he had made a national reputation, had become the recognized leader of his party, and had grown more self-confident and arrogant than ever; while the former [Lincoln], his party being in a minority in the State, had been in public life for only a brief period, had devoted himself almost exclusively to the labors of his profession [as a lawyer], and had no claims to a national reputation.

[Thus, the politically retired Mr. Lincoln seemed unlikely to do well in debate.] Douglas, through his newspaper organs and street trumpeters, a class to whom no man is more greatly indebted for his reputation, had contrived to create an impression in the minds of many people that he had grown to proportions too gigantic to render it safe for so unpretending and modest a man as Lincoln to encounter him.

[On October 3, 1854] Douglas entered upon the debate in this spirit [at the Illinois State Fair]. He displayed all of his most offensive peculiarities. He was arrogant, insolent, defiant, and throughout his speech maintained the air of one who had already conquered. On the next day, Lincoln replied. No report [i.e., no verbatim transcript] was made of either of the speeches; but the following extract from the Springfield *Journal* of the following day (October 6),[1] will show how Lincoln acquitted himself, and how greatly Douglas had overestimated his own abilities, and underrated those of his antagonist:

[Mr. Lincoln Denounces Kansas-Nebraska Act]

"[At the Illinois State Fair on October 4, 1854, Abraham Lincoln replied to Stephen Douglas.] Mr. Lincoln commenced at two o'clock, P.M., and spoke three hours and ten minutes. We [the reporters of this newspaper] propose to give our views and those of many Northerners and many Southerners upon the debate. We intend to give it as fairly as we can.

---

[1]   October 6 was *two* days after Mr. Lincoln spoke on October 4, 1854.

Protest!
October 27, 1854

Abraham Lincoln warned that
the expansion of slavery threat-
ened the Northern Free States.

Tarbell, 1896

"Those who know Mr. Lincoln, know him to be a conscientious and honest man, who makes no assertions that he does not know to be true. This anti-Nebraska speech of Mr. Lincoln [denouncing the Kansas-Nebraska Act of Senator Douglas], was the profoundest, in our opinion, that he has made in his whole life. He felt upon his soul;[1] the truths burn which he uttered; and all present felt that he was true to his own soul. His feelings once or twice swelled within and came near stifling utterance, and particularly so, when he said that the Declaration of Independence taught us that 'all men are created equal'—that by the laws of nature and nature's God, all men were free—that the Nebraska Law chained men [by expanding slavery into the West], and that there was as much difference between the glorious truths of the immortal Declaration of Independence and the Nebraska bill, as there was between God and Mammon.[2]

"These are his own words. They were spoken with emphasis, feeling and true eloquence; eloquent because true, and because he felt, and felt deeply, what he said. We only wish oth-

---

[1] *Felt upon his soul,* i.e.,. spoke forcefully from the heart.

[2] *Mammon* is a derogatory biblical term for money.

ers all over the State had seen him while uttering those truths only as Lincoln can utter a felt and deeply felt truth. He quivered with feeling and emotion. The whole house was as still as death. He attacked the Nebraska bill with unusual warmth and energy, and all felt that a man of strength was its enemy, and that he intended to blast it, if he could, by strong and manly efforts. He was most successful, and the house approved the glorious triumph of truth by loud and continued "Huzzahs!" Women waved their white handkerchiefs in token of woman's silent but heartfelt assent.

"[Stephen] Douglas felt the sting. He frequently interrupted Mr. Lincoln.[1] His friends felt that he was crushed by Lincoln's powerful argument, manly logic, and illustrations from nature around us. The Nebraska bill was shivered and, like a tree of the forest, was torn and rent asunder by the hot bolts of truth.

"Mr. Lincoln exhibited Douglas in all the attitudes he could be placed in a friendly debate. He exhibited the bill in all its aspects, to show its humbuggery and falsehoods; and when thus torn to rags, cut into slips, held up to the gaze of the vast crowd, a kind of scorn and mockery was visible upon the face of the crowd, and upon the lips of the most eloquent speaker. It was a proud day for Lincoln. His friends will never forget it.

"Nowhere in the whole speech of Mr. Lincoln, was he more grand than at the conclusion. He said this people [who expanded slavery] were degenerating from the sires of the [American] Revolution—from Washington, Jefferson, Madison, and Monroe —as it appeared to him;[2] yet he called upon the spirit of the brave, valiant free sons of all and every clime, to defend freedom and the institutions that our fathers and [George] Washington gave us;[3] and that now was the time to show to the world that we were not rolling back towards despotism.

---

[1] At Mr. Lincoln's invitation, Mr. Douglas sat in the first row of the audience.

[2] He echoes Frederick Douglass's charge of "degeneracy." See note, page 114.

[3] Mr. Lincoln subtly alludes to George Washington voluntarily freeing his own slaves, an act of conscience that still dismayed many slaveholders in 1860.

"At the conclusion of this speech, every man and child felt that it was unanswerable, that no human power could overthrow it or trample it under foot. The long and repeated applause evinced the feelings of the crowd, and gave token of universal assent to Lincoln's whole argument; and every mind present did homage to the man who took captive the heart and broke like a sun over the understanding."

The following extract is taken from an account of the same debate, given by the Chicago *Press and Tribune*:

"It would be impossible, in these limits, to give an idea of the strength of Mr. Lincoln's argument. We deemed it by far the ablest effort of the campaign—from whatever source. The occasion was a great one, and the speaker was every way equal to it. The effect produced on the listeners was magnetic. No one who was present will ever forget the power and vehemence of the following passage [uttered by Mr. Lincoln]:

"'My distinguished friend [Mr. Douglas] says it is an insult to the emigrants to Kansas and Nebraska to suppose they are not able to govern themselves. We must not slur over an argument of this kind because it happens to tickle the ear. It must be met and answered. I admit that the emigrant to Kansas and Nebraska is competent to govern *himself*, but ...' (the speaker rising to his full height) ... '*I deny his right to govern any other person* WITHOUT THAT PERSON'S CONSENT.'

"The applause which followed this triumphant refutation of a cunning falsehood, was but an earnest [or portent] of the victory at the polls which followed just one month from that day.

"When Mr. Lincoln had concluded, Mr. Douglas strode hastily to the stand. As usual, he employed ten minutes in telling how grossly he had been abused. Recollecting himself, he added, 'though in a perfectly courteous manner'—abused in a perfectly courteous manner!

"He then devoted half an hour to showing that it was indispensably necessary to California emigrants, Santa Fe traders and others, to have organic acts [federal laws creating local government] provided for the Territories of Kansas and Nebraska—that being precisely the point which nobody disputed. Having established this premise to his satisfaction, Mr. Douglas launched forth into an argument wholly apart from the positions taken by Mr. Lincoln. He had about half finished at six o'-clock, when an adjournment to tea was effected. The speaker insisted strenuously upon his right to resume in the evening, but we believe the second part of that speech has not been delivered to this day."

From Springfield, the parties went to Peoria [on October 16, 1854], where they again discussed the Kansas-Nebraska bill. On this occasion, the triumph of Mr. Lincoln was even more marked than at Springfield. His speech occupied over three hours in the delivery; and so masterly was it in argument, so crushing in its sarcasm, so compact in its logic, that Mr. Douglas did not even undertake to reply to the points raised by Mr. Lincoln. It was a thorough and unanswerable exposition of all the sophisms and plausible pretenses with which Douglas, up to that time, had invested the Kansas-Nebraska bill, and he stood before the audience in the attitude of a mountebank,[1] whose tricks are clearly seen through, by those whom he attempts to deceive.

Mr. Lincoln's speech on this occasion was reported [with a verbatim transcript]. As a specimen of the manner in which he drove Douglas to the wall on every point, take the following extract [preceded by a brief summary of Douglas's argument]:

Douglas had urged that the question of slavery in a Territory concerned only the people of the Territory—that it could be of no interest to the people of Illinois whether slavery was "voted up or voted down" in Kansas. To this Lincoln replied that, in the first place, the whole nation is interested that the best use shall be

---

[1]   A fraud or con artist who utters falsehoods from a podium.

Alfred Lawrence, August 1913/Library of Congress

Bleeding Kansas, 50th Anniversary, 1913
In a bittersweet reunion, survivors of the Lawrence Massacre of 1863 gather af-
ter half a century. Proslavery guerrillas killed 150 relatives and friends. The town
defiantly sheltered escaped black slaves, now pictured here as free citizens.

made of all the Territories [the new lands of the American West],
and that this end can alone be reached by preserving them as
homes for free white people[1] [and forbidding new slave planta-
tions]. His other point was the following, and certainly a more conclusive and unanswerable argument has never been uttered:

[Slavery Harms Free States]
"By the Constitution, each State has two senators. Each
[State] has a number of representatives [in the lower House of
Congress] in proportion to the number of its people; and each
has a number of presidential electors, equal to the whole num-

---

[1] Mr. Lincoln sometimes paid lip service to a biased era. However, here he
only refers to a sad fact: In 1854, most European-descended Americans were
family farmers, but most African-Americans were enslaved on plantations. Mr.
Lincoln advocates reserving all new lands for family farms. This restricts plantations and pressures them to free slaves. Implicitly, freed slaves might someday
be family farmers too. He adds that "my ancient faith teaches me that 'all men
are created equal,' and that there can be no moral right in connection with one
man's making a slave of another." See page 166 for more on the issue of race.

ber of its senators and representatives together. But in ascertaining the number of the people for the purpose [of allocating congressmen], five slaves are counted as being equal to three whites. The slaves do not vote; they are only counted and so used as to swell the influence of the white people's votes.

"The practical effect of this is more aptly shown by a comparison of the States of South Carolina and Maine. South Carolina has six representatives [in Congress], and so has Maine; South Carolina has eight presidential electors, and so has Maine. This is precise equality so far; and of course they are equal in senators, each having two. Thus, in the control of the government, the two States are equals precisely.

"But how are they in the number of their white people? Maine has 581,813, while South Carolina his 274,567. Maine has twice as many as South Carolina, and 32,679 over. Thus, each white man in South Carolina is more than the double of any man in Maine. This is all because South Carolina, besides her free people, has 384,984 slaves.

"The South Carolinian has precisely the same advantage over the white man in every other Free State [which bans slavery], as well as in Maine. He is more than the double of any one of us. The same advantage, but not to the same extent, is held by all the citizens of the slave States,[1] over those of the free; and it is absolute truth, without an exception, that there is no voter in any slave State [who is not so advantaged]—but who has more legal power in the government than any voter in any Free State. There is no instance of exact equality, and the disadvantage is against us the whole chapter through. This principle, in the aggregate, gives the slave States in the present Congress twenty additional representatives—being seven more than the whole majority by which they passed the Nebraska bill.

"Now all this is manifestly unfair; yet I do not mention it to complain of it, in so far as it is already settled. It is in the Constitution, and I do not, for that cause, or any other cause, propose to destroy, or alter, or disregard the Constitution; I stand to it fairly, fully, and firmly. But when I am told that I must leave it altogether to *other people* to say whether new partners are to be bred up and brought into the firm on the same degrading terms against me,[2] I respectfully demur. I insist that whether I shall be a whole man, or only the half of one in comparison with others, is a question in which I am somewhat concerned; and one which no other man can have a 'sacred right' of deciding for me.

"If I am wrong in this, if it really be a 'sacred right' of self-government in the man who shall go to Nebraska——to decide whether he will be the equal of me or the double of me—then after he shall have exercised that right, and thereby shall have reduced me to a still smaller fraction of a man than I already am, I should like for some gentleman deeply skilled in the mysteries of 'sacred rights' to provide himself with a microscope, and peep about and find out if he can, what has become of *my* 'sacred rights?'—They will surely be too small for detection with the naked eye.

---

[1] Mr. Lincoln pointedly never capitalizes *slave States,* only *Free States.*

[2] Mr. Lincoln, a lawyer, likens *States* to partners in a law firm. Existing partners never surrender privileges to new partners.

"Finally, I insist that if there is anything which it is the duty of the *whole people* to never entrust to any hands but their own, that thing is the preservation in perpetuity of their own liberties and institutions. And if they shall think, as I do, that the extension of slavery endangers them more than any, or all other causes, how recreant[1] to themselves if they submit the question, and with it, the fate of their country, to a mere handful of men bent only on temporary self-interest! If this question of slavery extension were an insignificant one—one having no power to do harm—it might be shuffled aside in this way. But being as it is the great Behemoth of danger, shall the strong grip[2] of the nation be loosened upon him, to entrust him to the hands of such feeble keepers?"

It was Mr. Lincoln's purpose and desire to continue the discussion with Mr. Douglas during the remainder of the canvass [in the autumn of 1854], but that gentleman shrank from a repetition of the discomfiture he had suffered at Springfield and Peoria. He gave Mr. Lincoln no further opportunity of meeting him.

But notwithstanding his antagonist withdrew from the unequal contest, Mr. Lincoln continued in the field. He pressed the slavery issue—which the repeal of the Missouri Compromise had forced upon the country—upon the people of central and southern Illinois (who were largely made up of emigrants from Kentucky, Tennessee, Virginia and North Carolina [all slave States]) with all the powers of his mind. He felt the force of the moral causes that must influence the final settlement of the question, and he never failed to appeal to the moral sentiment of the people, in aid of the argument drawn from political sources, and to illuminate his theme with the lofty inspirations of true eloquence pleading for the rights of humanity.

[His speeches transformed the 1854 election.] A revolution swept the State: For the first time since the organization of the Democratic Party, a majority of those elected to the legislature of Illinois

---

[1] *Recreant* is a synonym for disloyal or unfaithful.

[2] *Grip* replaces the archaic *gripe* in the 1860 text.

were opposed to the Democratic administration of the federal government [then led by President Franklin Pierce, an ally of slaveholders].

(While Mr. Lincoln was engaged in the canvass in other parts of the State, his friends in Sangamon County, without his consent or knowledge, presented his name for the legislature, and he was elected to that body by a handsome majority. It was not in his power to serve,[1] and he was compelled to decline the well-meant honor conferred upon him by the people of Sangamon.)

[The New Antislavery Opposition]

[A majority of the new Illinois legislature of 1854 disapproved of Senator Douglas's policy on slavery.] This was Lincoln's first triumph over Douglas in an appeal to the people of the State. His second triumph occurred two years later in the election of the entire Republican state ticket [on an antislavery platform], and his third was in the memorable senatorial contest of 1858, when his majority over Douglas exceeded 4,000 votes [of 251,148 cast].

[Nevertheless, even after losing many districts in 1854, Democrats loyal to Mr. Douglas were still the largest single bloc in the Illinois legislature. Antislavery forces were not yet unified.] The Opposition in the legislature was made up of Whigs, Americans [the self-styled name of a third party],[2] and Anti-Nebraska Democrats. (The Republican Party was not organized in Illinois until 1856, two years later.)

These three divisions of the Opposition had no common platform, except that of hostility to the repeal of the Missouri Compromise, and to the revolutionary principles of the Kansas-Nebraska bill. The Old Whigs were still looking for a revival of their own organization. The Anti-Nebraska Democrats [the antislavery protesters of their party] had not abandoned the hope that the repeal of the Missouri Compromise and the principles of the Kansas-Nebraska bill would yet be repudiated by the Democratic Party.

---

[1] Mr. Lincoln plans to run for U.S. senator. The Illinois Constitution barred state legislators from being senators, because at the time the former elected the latter. Only after 1913 were U.S. senators elected by direct vote of the people.

[2] *Americans* was the self-styled name of an anti-immigrant faction, also called the Know-Nothings. Mr. Lincoln abhorred their bias and kept his distance.

James Shields (1810-79)
Longtime Lincoln Foe
U.S. Senator, D-Ill., 1849-55

When they were young, he challenged Mr.
Lincoln to a duel. Friends dissuaded them.

Library of Congress

[Turning Point, Elections of 1854-55]

[Editor's Note: The elections in 1854 for the Illinois state legislature were a pivotal event. Up to that year, a Democratic Party allied with Southern slaveholders dominated Illinois and other Midwestern States. After 1854, an antislavery movement calling itself *Republican* took root.

In 1855, this shift upended the U.S. Senate race in Illinois. The incumbent Democrat James Shields was suddenly vulnerable as an ally of Stephen Douglas. (The latter was not up for reelection until 1858.) Mr. Lincoln ran against Senator Shields as a Whig, but protests also arose *within* Mr. Shields's own Democratic Party. Antislavery legislators bolted and formed a separate faction. Old-line Democrats lost their longtime majority in the Illinois state legislature, which, at the time, picked U.S. senators.

The dissenting Democrats were a portent of the future. They previously accepted slavery, so long as it only affected *other* people in far-away places, e.g., the Deep South. However, Senator Douglas and old-line Democrats allowed slavery to spread into nearby frontier Territories such as Kansas and Nebraska. Mr. Douglas coolly claimed indifference, but many people in Illinois (where slavery was banned) were alarmed. Cutthroat competition from a neighboring slave economy could overwhelm local farms and businesses.

Large numbers of voters now viewed slavery as a threat to *themselves*, not just to the slaves. The change in public opinion unexpectedly gave the retired Mr. Lincoln a second chance in politics at age 45. He was motivated by moral principle—against slavery—and by animosity with incumbent Senator James Shields—they once almost fought a duel to the death.[1] It was one of the few times that Abraham Lincoln mixed politics with old scores.]

---

[1] In 1842, Mr. Lincoln published a satire, accusing James Shields of vanity. The latter sought a duel; the former agreed to swords. Friends dissuaded them.

[Illinois Legislature Meets, February 1855]

[When the new Illinois legislature gathered in early 1855, Mr. Lincoln's Whigs discussed a possible alliance with the antislavery Democrats.] When the election of a United States senator came on, the latter declined going into caucus with the Opposition; they had never acted politically with the Whigs as a party. To preserve their identity, to be able to exert a due influence on the Democratic Party, and to force it into the abandonment of its new and dangerous dogmas, they [the antislavery Democrats] believed sound policy required them to nominate and adhere to one of their own number.

The remainder of the Opposition went into caucus and nominated Mr. Lincoln [for U.S. senator]. When the two houses [the State Senate and House of Representatives] met in joint session, February 8, 1855, the Whigs presented the name of Abraham Lincoln; the Anti-Nebraska Democrats [against slavery], that of Lyman Trumbull;[1] the Democrats [loyal to Mr. Douglas], that of General James Shields.

The whole number of votes [in the legislature] was 99, of which 50 were necessary to a choice [for U.S. senator]. On the first ballot, the vote stood for Abraham Lincoln 45; James Shields 41; for Lyman Trumbull 5; scattering 8. On the seventh ballot, the Democrats dropped General Shields and voted for Joel A. Matteson, [a Democrat] then holding the office of governor of the State.

Governor Matteson had never openly taken ground for, or against the Kansas-Nebraska bill. He was a shrewd man, and had long been arranging and planning for the emergency which had now occurred. On the seventh ballot (first for him) he received 44 votes, two higher than Shields had at any time received; on the eighth he received 46 votes, and on the ninth, 47, or within three of an election. On that ballot, for the second time, the joint vote of Lincoln and Trumbull [an antislavery Democrat] was just sufficient to elect [and decide the Senate race], if thrown for a single person, viz., for Trumbull 35, for Lincoln 15—and this, too, was the first time that Trumbull's vote had exceeded Lincoln's.

---

[1] Lyman Trumbull (1813-96) later joined the antislavery Republican Party and supported President Lincoln during the Civil War.

Lyman Trumbull (1813-96)
Antislavery Protester
U.S. Senator, D-, R-Ill., 1855-73

He deserted the Democratic Party's alliance with slaveholders. Stephen Douglas branded him a turncoat.

Library of Congress

[Mr. Lincoln then sacrificed his candidacy to unify the antislavery vote.] Perceiving the danger of electing Matteson, unless his own and Trumbull's strength could be united at once, Lincoln went to his friends and begged them to cast their united vote on the next ballot for Trumbull. They yielded to his urgent entreaties, and on the next ballot, Mr. Trumbull received 51 votes and was declared elected [as U.S. senator].

The scene will long be remembered by those who witnessed it. The excitement was most intense. The Democrats [loyal to Mr. Douglas] had never doubted their ability to elect some noncommittal man like Matteson. They did not believe the Opposition could be brought to unite. They were not prepared for such a display of magnanimity as that exhibited by Mr. Lincoln. The result filled them with astonishment as well as chagrin.

On the other hand, the old political associates of Mr. Lincoln felt that he was entitled to the place [as senator], and that all portions of the Opposition ought to have united in awarding it to him. Strong men wept at the necessity which required them to withdraw their votes from him. He alone was calm and unmoved, in the midst of all these different phases of excitement.

Zealous efforts have since been made to awaken unkind feelings on the part of Mr. Lincoln against Senator Trumbull and those

Anti-Nebraska Democrats who brought him forward as a candidate; but all to no purpose. The relations subsisting between him and them were of the most frank and cordial character at the time, and such they have been over since. He justly ranks them among his best friends; and surely none have gone or can go beyond them in manifestation of zeal in his behalf, both as a candidate for the Senate in 1858, and for the presidency in 1860.

[Antislavery Republicans Established]

[Editor's Note: Abraham Lincoln's antislavery alliance with former opponents in the Illinois Democratic Party was mirrored in other Northern States. Longtime partisan foes, Whigs and dissenting Democrats, joined "fusion" tickets to defeat proslavery Democrats. By 1856, this ad hoc coalition formed a new political party, the Republicans. Mr. Lincoln's traditional Whig Party disappeared, and Illinois joined an historic national realignment.]

In June 1856, a convention of those opposed to the Democratic Party was held at Bloomington, Illinois, at which time the Republican Party was organized in that State, a platform adopted, a state ticket nominated, and delegates appointed to the National Republican Convention to meet at Philadelphia.[1] Mr. Lincoln bore a leading part in securing these results. Perhaps no other man exerted so wide and salutary an influence in harmonizing differences, in softening and obliterating prejudices, and bringing into a cordial union those who for years had been bitterly hostile to each other.

His speech before that Convention [of Illinois State Republicans in Bloomington] will ever be regarded by many of those who heard it, as the greatest effort of his life.[2] Never was an audience more completely electrified by human eloquence. Again and again, during the progress of its delivery, they sprang to their feet and upon the benches, and testified—by long-continued shouts and the waving of hats—how deeply the speaker had wrought upon their minds and hearts. It fused the mass of hitherto incongruous elements [of the new party] into perfect homogeneity, and from that day to the

---

[1]   The State Convention convened May 29, 1856; the National, June 17, 1856.

[2]   Historians dub his 1856 oration as "the Lost Speech," because no transcript was made, and Mr. Lincoln refused to supply a written copy. He worried that he may have gone too far in a fiery denunciation of slavery and its supporters.

Firebrand
1857

Alexander Hesler of Chicago pho-
tographed a "homey" Mr. Lincoln.

Tarbell, 1907

present, they have worked together in harmonious and fraternal union. It kindled also an enthusiasm in the bosoms of those who heard it—[a political fervor] which they carried home with them, and with which they imbued their neighbors, and by which the Republican Party of Illinois, in the first year of its existence [1856], was carried triumphantly into power [winning state offices].

At the National Republican Convention of that year, Mr. Lincoln's name was presented by the Western delegates for nomination for the vice presidency [of the United States]. Although had his own wishes been consulted in the matter, he would not have consented to this use of his name, it was nevertheless a well-deserved compliment, as well as a recognition of the fact that his reputation had now become national. Mr. Lincoln's vote on the informal ballot was 110 [delegates]; Mr. Dayton's, 259.

[Editor's Note: Former U.S. Senator William L. Dayton of New Jersey won the 1856 Republican nomination for vice president. For the runner-up Mr. Lincoln, it was a blessing in disguise. Mr. Dayton joined the losing presidential ticket of John C. Frémont, an explorer and soldier turned politician. James Buchanan, an ally of slaveholders, trounced them to become the fifteenth president of the United States. In the next election, that of 1860, antislavery voters sought fresh candidates untainted by the loss, e.g., Mr. Lincoln.]

[Disputing the Declaration of Independence]

During the recess of Congress in 1857, Mr. Douglas made a speech at Springfield in further vindication of his Kansas-Nebraska bill, known as his "Grand Jury Speech," from the fact that he was invited to deliver it by the Grand Jury of the U.S. District Court for Southern Illinois. In that speech, he first promulgated the doctrine that the framers of the Declaration of Independence, in asserting that "all men are created equal," simply meant to say that "British subjects on this continent were equal to British subjects born and residing in Great Britain."

Mr. Lincoln, by invitation of a large number of his fellow citizens, replied to Douglas. When he came to that part of the speech which contained his (Douglas's) theory of the Declaration, as above given, Mr. Lincoln said:

[Mocking Mr. Douglas]

"My good friends, read that [opinion by Mr. Douglas] carefully over some leisure hour, and ponder well upon it. See what a mere wreck—a mangled ruin—it makes of our glorious Declaration! [Mr. Douglas says] they were speaking of British subjects on this continent being equal to British subjects born and residing in Great Britain! Why, according to this, not only Negroes, but white people outside of Great Britain and America were not spoken of in that instrument. The English, Irish, and Scotch, along with white Americans, were included to be sure, but the French, Germans, and other white people of the world are all gone to pot along with the Judge's inferior races.[1]

"I had thought the Declaration promised something better than the condition of British subjects; but no, it only meant that we should be *equal* to them in their own oppressed and *unequal* condition. According to that, it gave no promise that, having kicked off the King and Lords of Great Britain, we should not at once be saddled with a King and Lords of our own.

---

[1] Mr. Douglas slurred blacks and "any other inferior or degraded race." "Judge" refers to a former stint as a Justice on the Illinois State Supreme Court.

"I had thought the Declaration contemplated a progressive improvement in the condition of all men everywhere; but no, [Mr. Douglas says] it merely 'was adopted for the purpose of justifying the colonists in the eyes of the civilized world in withdrawing their allegiance from the British crown, and dissolving their connection with the mother country.' Why, that object having been effected some eighty years ago, the Declaration is of no practical use now—mere rubbish, old wadding left to rot on the battlefield after the victory is won.

"I understand you are preparing to celebrate the 'Fourth [of July],' tomorrow week. What for? [Mr. Douglas says] the doings of that day had no reference to the present; and quite half of you are not even descendants of those who were referred to at that day. But I suppose you will celebrate, and will even go so far as to read the Declaration. Suppose after you read it once in the old-fashioned way, you read it once more with Judge Douglas's version. It will then run thus: 'We hold these truths to be self-evident, that all British subjects who were on this continent eighty-one years ago, were created equal to all British subjects born and *then* residing in Great Britain.'

"And now, I appeal to all—to Democrats [led by Mr. Douglas] as well as others—are you really willing that the Declaration shall thus be frittered away?—thus left no more, at most, than an interesting memorial of the dead past?—thus shorn of its vitality and practical value, and left without the *germ*, or even the *suggestion*, of the inalienable rights of man in it?"

Mr. Lincoln then gave his own views of the intention of the framers of the Declaration; and in the contrast between his theory and that of Douglas, the relative moral and philosophic status of the two men is most clearly shown. This is Mr. Lincoln's theory:

[The Progress of Human Rights]

"I think the authors of that notable instrument [the Declaration of Independence] intended to include *all* men, but they did not intend to declare all men equal *in all respects*. They did not mean to say all were equal in color, size, intellect, moral development, or social capacity. They defined, with tolerable distinctness, in what respects they did consider all men created equal—equal in "certain inalienable rights, among which are life, liberty, and the pursuit of happiness." This they said, and this they meant.

"They did not mean to assert the obvious untruth that all were then actually enjoying that equality, nor yet that they were about to confer it immediately upon them. In fact, they had no power to confer such a boon. They meant simply to declare the *right*, so that the *enforcement* of it might follow as fast as circumstance should permit.

"*They meant to set up a standard maxim for free society, which should be familiar to all, and revered by all; constantly looked to, constantly labored for, and even though never perfectly attained, constantly approximated, and thereby constantly spreading and deepening its influence, and augmenting the happiness and value of life to all people of all colors everywhere.*

"The assertion that 'all men are created equal' was of no practical use in effecting our separation from Great Britain; and it was placed in the Declaration not for that, but for future use. Its authors meant it to be as, thank God, it is now proving itself, a stumbling block to all those who in aftertimes might seek to turn a free people back into the hateful paths of despotism. They knew the proneness of prosperity to breed tyrants, and they meant when such should reappear in this fair land and commence their vocation, they should find left for them at least one hard nut to crack."

[These are Mr. Lincoln's and Mr. Douglas's differing views of the Declaration of Independence.] Let the reader decide on which theory the heroes of the [American] Revolution, are most entitled to the veneration of posterity—on which the assertion and defense of the natural and inalienable rights of man can be most successfully maintained.

Chapter Nine [Eight]¹
The Senatorial Contest with Douglas in 1858

The Democratic State Convention met at Springfield on the twenty-first of April 1858, and published a declaration of the principles on which they proposed to make their battle [to reelect their leader, incumbent U.S. Senator Stephen Douglas]. They resolved:

> "That the Democracy of Illinois [aka the Democratic Party] are unalterably attached to, and will maintain inviolate, *the principles declared in the National Democratic Convention at Cincinnati in June 1856* [and which formed the campaign platform of their presidential nominee, James Buchanan of Pennsylvania]."²

Several supplementary resolutions were adopted, all tending to the same conclusion. [Editor's Note: In 1856, the Cincinnati platform of the Democratic Party reiterated the principles of the Kansas-Nebraska Act of 1854. Slavery could expand into new Territories of the American West, if "popular sovereignty" so dictated, i.e., local settlers voted for slavery. In practice, armed partisans sought to force slavery into frontier lands.

Nevertheless, in the 1856 election, Democrat James Buchanan won the presidency, defeating John C. Frémont, the antislavery Republican. Once in office, Mr. Buchanan cheerfully sent to Congress a new constitution for frontier Kansas. This "Lecompton" Constitution openly backed slavery.]

Senator Douglas and his Democratic colleagues in the House of Representatives were warmly endorsed [at their 1858 State Convention], and promised the "earnest and efficient support" of the party in the coming campaign. No rebuke was offered to the administration [of then President Buchanan] for its course on Lecompton, except by a misty inference. The last resolution was as follows:

> "*Resolved*, That in all things wherein the National Administration sustain and carry out the principles of the Democratic Party, as expressed in the Cincinnati platform and affirmed in their resolutions, it is entitled to, and will receive our hearty support."

---

¹ This is the eighth chapter. Chapter numbers in the 1860 text are inaccurate.

² Mr. Buchanan was president, 1857-61, just before Abraham Lincoln.

[Antislavery Republican Convention, 1858]

The distinct and unqualified endorsement of the Cincinnati platform by the friends of Mr. Douglas, their neglect to pass any censure on the corruptions and tergiversations[1] of President Buchanan, and their violent speeches in the Convention against the Republicans [the new antislavery party], destroyed whatever hope of union and compromise might have been entertained by members of either party.

The challenge had passed, and the Republicans were not slow in accepting it. Their State Convention was held at Springfield on the sixteenth of June [1858], seven weeks later than the other. [Mr. Douglas's Democrats had met in April 1858.] Nearly one-thousand delegates and alternates were present, and the chairman of the committee on credentials reported fourteen-hundred persons in attendance, other than the resident population of the capital.

It was very soon ascertained that the [Republican] Convention was *all for Lincoln* [to be its candidate for U.S. senator]. Immediately after the organization [to establish nominating rules], a Chicago delegate brought into the hall a banner on which were inscribed the words, "COOK COUNTY[2] FOR ABRAHAM LINCOLN." The whole Convention rose simultaneously and gave three cheers for the candidate upon whom it was proposed to confer the perilous honor of a nomination against Senator Douglas.

The precarious ground which Mr. Douglas's opposition to the Lecompton Constitution had left for a distinctive Republican candidate before the masses, was carefully considered by the committee on resolutions.

[Editor's Note: In 1857, Stephen Douglas abruptly repudiated the Lecompton Constitution, a contentious proposal to protect slavery in frontier Kansas. Senator Douglas was on the eve of his reelection campaign, but his move still surprised many. *He* had championed the changes in federal law that made slavery possible in Kansas.

Public opinion, though, had shifted. Senator Douglas now presented himself as a sometimes ally of "free soil," i.e., keeping slavery *out* of new Ter-

---

[1]   A *tergiversation* is a betrayal or desertion of long-held principles.

[2]   Cook County is the most populous county of Illinois and includes Chicago.

ritories. In December 1857, Mr. Douglas suddenly rebuked President Buchanan, a fellow Democrat, for praising the proslavery Lecompton plan. Senator Douglas's newfound opposition to *some* slavery muddied the political
waters for a challenger of longstanding antislavery views, e.g., Mr. Lincoln.]

[Confusion]

[Some antislavery voters in Illinois accepted Stephen Douglas's
eleventh-hour conversion.] The alleged sympathy entertained for him
by prominent Republicans in other parts of the country; the odor of
free soil which he had collected in his garments during the recent
session of Congress—notwithstanding his obstinate and blind adher-
ence to the *Dred Scott* decision [a court case legalizing slavery in
new Territories];[1] the universal favor to which he had been com-
mended by the persecutions of the administration [of President
Buchanan];[2] the flagrant apportionment of the State into legislative
districts by which ninety-three thousand people in the Republican
counties were virtually disfranchised—combined to give a very unpromising complexion to the campaign.

Nothing was to be done, however, but to lay down a platform of
straight Republican principles [opposed to the expansion of slavery]
and trust to their potency, and the popularity of their leader [Mr.
Lincoln], for a successful issue. It was agreed that any result was
to be courted, rather than allow the Republican Party to become
the tail for a kite patched together from the Cincinnati platform [of
Mr. Douglas's Democrats] and the *Dred Scott* decision.

The Convention [the 1858 meeting of Illinois Republicans] then
proceeded to the adoption of a platform of principles, and the nomination of candidates for state treasurer and superintendent of public instruction. It was not deemed advisable by the committee on
resolutions to give Mr. Lincoln a formal nomination for the Senate
[because his antislavery views might be *too* forceful], but many
members of the convention deemed it proper to do so, in order to
destroy the force of allegations, which had already been put forth

---

[1]   Detailed discussion about *Dred Scott,* an 1857 case, appears later in the text.

[2]   President Buchanan retaliated against Mr. Douglas for switching sides on
Kansas. Friends lost federal jobs;Mr. Douglas later lost a Senate chairmanship.

by Mr. Douglas from his seat in the Senate, that the Republicans designed to elect a different man [not Mr. Lincoln], provided they were successful in securing a majority of the legislature.

[Editor's Note: At the time, elections for U.S. senator were indirect. Voters elected a political party to control the state legislature, which then chose a senator. Mr. Douglas charged that the Republicans, if they won the Illinois legislature, planned to renege, and *not* pick Mr. Lincoln.

The charge was not implausible. Mr. Lincoln's passionate antislavery views alienated many voters in Illinois, e.g., recent emigrants from slave States. Republicans in close districts might have second thoughts about being linked to him. As such, Mr. Douglas, supposedly a belated ally of "free soil," hinted he (Douglas) was a safer choice, rather than a last-minute substitute fobbed off by the Republicans. Even some antislavery activists, e.g., Horace Greeley, a major publisher in New York, then favored Mr. Douglas.]

The following resolution [at the Illinois Republican Convention] was therefore offered by a delegate, and adopted unanimously:

> "*Resolved,* That the Hon. Abraham Lincoln is our first and only choice for U.S. Senator, to fill the vacancy about to be created by the expiration of Mr. Douglas's term of office."

Mr. Lincoln had been frequently called for during the session [to speak], but did not make his appearance. The secretary of state [Ozias Hatch, the ranking Republican in Illinois], however, announced that if it was the desire of his friends, he [Lincoln] would address the members of the Convention in the Representatives' Hall [in the Old State House] in the evening, about 8 o'clock [June 16, 1858].

Therefore, the room was filled to its utmost capacity, and Mr. Lincoln spoke about half an hour. The limits of this work do not permit the introduction of any speeches at full length, but the masterly manner in which the pending topics were discussed, the wide celebrity which this speech acquired, and more especially the fact that it contained the *essence* of the whole campaign, require that more than a passing notice should be given to it. The exceeding terseness of all Mr. Lincoln's efforts renders it difficult to condense his utterances without impairing or destroying their force, yet the reader will be able to catch the essential points of his argument from the following summary.

[The House Divided]

[Editor's Note: The following is an excerpt of the famed "House Divided" speech, which began Mr. Lincoln's meteoric rise to the presidency. Before he delivered it on June 16, 1858, he was, at best, only a regional figure. Afterwards, he was a celebrity in antislavery circles throughout America.

Mr. Lincoln, though, was still not a leading presidential contender. Senator William Seward, R-N.Y., the urbane former governor of New York, remained the front-runner to head the antislavery ticket in 1860. However, some thought Mr. Seward reckless; in October 1858, he stunned many with talk of "irrepressible conflict."

By contrast, in his "House Divided" speech, Mr. Lincoln is a pacifist. He rejects the notion that the United States might be dissolved—the peace may yet be preserved. Yet Mr. Lincoln also stirs a hornets' nest: He warns that slavery might sweep the nation, overturning local laws of Free States.]

We quote the opening paragraph entire[ly]:

"MR. PRESIDENT, AND GENTLEMEN OF THE CONVENTION [the 1858 convocation of Illinois State Republicans]:

"If we could first know where we are, and whither we are tending, we could better judge what to do, and how to do it. We are now in the fifth year since a policy [the Kansas-Nebraska Act of 1854] was initiated with the avowed object, and confident promise, of putting an end to slavery agitation. Under the operation of that policy, that agitation has not only not ceased, but has constantly augmented. In my opinion, it will not cease, until a crisis shall have been reached and passed. 'A house divided against itself cannot stand.' I believe this government cannot endure permanently half slave and half free.

"I do not expect the Union [the national existence of the United States] to be dissolved—I do not expect the house to fall —but I do expect it will cease to be divided. It will become all one thing, or all the other. Either the opponents of slavery will arrest the further spread of it, and place it where the public mind shall rest in the belief that it is in the course of ultimate extinction; or its advocates will push it forward, till it shall become alike lawful in all the States, Old as well as New—North as well as South.

"Have we no tendency to the latter condition?

Oldroyd, 1896

Old State House, Springfield
Site of "House Divided" Speech, June 16, 1858

"Let anyone who doubts, carefully contemplate that now almost complete legal combination—piece of machinery, so to
speak—compounded of the [Kansas]-Nebraska doctrine, and
the *Dred Scott* decision [a court case legalizing slavery in new
Territories of the West]. Let him consider not only what work
the machinery is adapted to, and how well adapted; but also,
let him study the history of its construction, and trace, if he
can—or rather fail, if he can—to trace the evidences of design,
in concert of action among its chief architects from the beginning."

Mr. Lincoln then proceeded to show that prior to 1854, slavery
had been excluded from more than half the *States* by local laws or
constitutions, and from the greater portion of the national territory
by congressional prohibition [barring slavery in most new lands of
the West]. On the fourth of January 1854, the struggle commenced
[when Senator Douglas introduced his Kansas-Nebraska Act],
which ended with the repeal of the congressional prohibition, accomplished on the grounds of squatter sovereignty, and "sacred
right of self-government," which meant that "if any *one* man choos-
es to enslave *another*, no *third* man shall be allowed to object."

The Conspiracy of "Slave Power"

Mr. Lincoln's "House Divided" speech of 1858 caused a national uproar. A conspiracy, he warned, sought to overturn the traditional right of Americans to prohibit slavery in their own communities. His warning intensified concern about a sinister "slave power."

Mr. Lincoln cited as evidence the congressional repeal of the Missouri Compromise, which had reserved most of the American West for family farmers; the Dred Scott *decision of the Supreme Court, which ended all restrictions on slavery in new U.S. Territories; and a suspected future Court decision that would impose slavery on existing States, regardless of local law and custom.*

Changes in the economy underscored these political events. Slaveholders experimented with factories manned by slaves, undercutting high-wage industries of Free States. Ruthless competition could force all Americans to the level of impoverished slaves.

This is shown to be a correct definition by the fact that when Mr. Chase [Free Soil-Ohio] in the Senate, and Mr. Mace [D-Ind.] in the House of Representatives,[1] offered their amendments to the Kansas-Nebraska bill [or the Nebraska bill for short], declaring that the people of the Territories might *exclude* slavery if they wanted to, Mr. Douglas and the other friends of the measure *voted them down.*

But while the Nebraska bill was going through Congress, the *Dred Scott* case was going through the courts [legalizing slavery in new Territories]; and when Senator Trumbull asked Senator Douglas whether, in his opinion, the people of a Territory could *exclude* slavery, the latter replied that it was "a question for the Supreme Court"—the Nebraska bill having provided that the rights of the people should be "subject to the Constitution of the United States." [Mr. Douglas seemed to know *in advance* that the Supreme

---

[1] U.S. Senator Salmon P. Chase and Representative Daniel H. Mace were antislavery leaders; Senator Chase (1808-73) then belonged to the Free Soil Party. In 1860, Mr. Chase ran for the Republican nomination for president, but finished behind Mr. Lincoln and William Seward.

The Dred Scott *Decision*

On March 6, 1857, the U.S. Supreme Court issued its infamous
Dred Scott *decision. The tribunal denied freedom to a black slave
named Dred Scott, even though he had resided in a frontier Territory
where Congress banned slavery. Chief Justice Roger Taney, a former
slaveholder, declared that black people were not U.S. citizens and
"had no rights which the white man was bound to respect; and ...
might justly and lawfully be reduced to slavery for his benefit."*

*In a problematic interpretation of the U.S. Constitution, the
Supreme Court also ended both federal and local bans on slavery in
the new Territories of the American West. Slavery could expand there
without restriction. Slaveholders rejoiced; antislavery activists were
appalled. Stephen Douglas and Abraham Lincoln heatedly took opposing sides, for and against the decision respectively.*

Court would use *Dred Scott* and the Constitution to block voters
from excluding slavery.]

[Several major actions followed:]

- The Nebraska bill was passed [in 1854] by both branches of
  Congress, and received the signature of the president;[1]
- The election of 1856 was carried by the Democracy [aka
  the Democratic Party], on the issue of "sacred right of self-
  government [to locally decide the slavery issue]"; and then
- The Supreme Court [in 1857] decided in the *Dred Scott* case
  that neither Congress *nor a territorial legislature* could exclude slavery from any United States Territory.

[Editor's Note: The net effect of the above events was always the same:
Restrictions on slavery ended in the federally supervised Territories of the
American West. Congress lost regulatory powers, but local settlers only gained
self-government to *approve* slavery. The Supreme Court forbade *all* bans on
slavery in the new Territories, nullifying even local laws. Hence, Mr. Lincoln
made his charge of conspiracy: Congress, two presidents, the Democratic Party, and the Supreme Court allegedly plotted an expansion of slavery.]

[By 1858, all federal bans on domestic slavery ceased. Only
some state laws still banned the practice.] But the *Dred Scott*

---

[1]   Franklin Pierce (1804-69), D-N.H., U.S. president, 1853-57.

judges refused to decide whether the holding of Dred Scott [a slave from Missouri] in the Free State of Illinois by his master, made him a free man. [I.e., the Supreme Court failed to confirm the validity of state laws banning slavery.] One member of the Court (Judge Nelson)[1] approached this branch of the case so nearly as to say that "except in cases where the power is restrained '*by the Constitution of the United States*,' the law of the State is supreme over the subject of slavery, within its jurisdiction."

In view of this strange decision, does it not appear that the phrase, "subject to the Constitution of the United States" in the [Kansas]-Nebraska bill, was interpolated for the purpose of leaving room for the *Dred Scott* decision [to artificially create a constitutional barrier to limiting slavery]? We quote again from Mr. Lincoln's words:

[Conspiracy to Spread Slavery]

"We cannot absolutely know that all these exact adaptations are the result of preconcert. But when we see a lot of framed timbers, different portions of which we know have been gotten out at different times and places, and by different workmen— Stephen, Franklin, Roger, and James, for instance[2]—and when we see these timbers joined together, and see they exactly make the frame of a house or a mill, all the tenons and mortices exactly fitting, and all the lengths and proportions of the different pieces exactly adapted to their respective places, and not a piece too many or too few—not omitting even scaffolding—or, if a single piece be lacking, we see the place in the frame exactly fitted and prepared yet to bring such piece in—in such a case, we find it impossible not to believe that Stephen and Franklin and Roger and James all understood one another from the beginning, and all worked upon a common plan or draft, drawn up before the first blow was struck."

---

[1] Justice Samuel Nelson (1792-1873) initially decided *Dred Scott* on a technicality. However, other Justices substituted a bellicose, racist defense of slavery.

[2] Thinly disguised allegory for *Stephen* Douglas; Presidents *Franklin* Pierce and *James* Buchanan; and *Roger* Taney, Chief Justice, U.S. Supreme Court.

James Buchanan (1791-1868)
U.S. President, 1857-61

In 1857, he expressed enthusiasm for
a proslavery constitution for the new
frontier Territory of Kansas.

Stephenson, 1921

[Forcing Slavery into Free States]

So far [the discussion was] as to *Territories* [those regions not yet States]. How as to States? Singularly enough, the [Kansas]-Nebraska bill said that it was "the true intent and meaning of this act not to legislate slavery into any Territory or *State*, nor to exclude it therefrom." Why was the word "State" employed?—the Nebraska conspirators were legislating for Territories, not States.

[Editor's Note: The implication is that Senator Douglas and his alleged co-conspirators plan to secretly force slavery into existing Free States, just as they would force it into new Territories of the West. Another Supreme Court decision, analogous to *Dred Scott,* might be the chosen instrument.]

It would seem from the ominous expression of Judge Nelson quoted above, as though a *second* niche had been left in the Nebraska bill, to be filled by a *second Dred Scott* decision—possibly the decision in the Lemmon case[1]—declaring that as no *Territory* can exclude slavery, neither can any *State*.

"And," says Mr. Lincoln, "this may especially be expected if the doctrine [by Senator Douglas] of 'care not whether slavery be voted down or voted up,' shall gain upon the public mind sufficiently to

---

[1] In 1852, New York State freed slaves held by Juliet Lemmon, a citizen of Virginia residing in New York. Many predicted the U.S. Supreme Court would overturn such state action, thereby forcing slavery into States that opposed it.

give promise that such a decision [to force slavery into unwilling States] can be maintained when made."

Such was Mr. Lincoln's admirable presentation of the issues of 1858. It is difficult to see in what point the argument is not equally good today [in 1860].

[Illinois Senate Campaign of 1858]

Mr. Douglas returned to Chicago [from the U.S. Senate in Washington] on the ninth of July [1858], and speedily realized the expectations of the Republicans of his own State by making a speech cordially and emphatically re-endorsing the *Dred Scott* decision. [The antislavery Republicans strongly disapproved of *Dred Scott*.]

On the twenty-fourth of July, Mr. Lincoln addressed the following note to his antagonist:

[Proposal to Debate]

"Hon. S. A. Douglas—*My Dear Sir:* Will it be agreeable to you to make an arrangement for you and myself to divide time, and address the same audiences during the present canvass? Mr. Judd,[1] who will hand you this, is authorized to receive your answer; and, if agreeable to you, to enter into the terms of such arrangement.
"Your obedient servant, A. LINCOLN."

Mr. Douglas had too vivid a recollection of his past encounters with Mr. Lincoln, to desire a repetition of them. Had he not felt in his inmost soul that Mr. Lincoln was more than a match for him in debate, he would not have waited for a challenge, but would himself have thrown down the glove to Mr. Lincoln immediately upon entering the State. His reply, declining the proposed arrangement [to make *all* campaign appearances together], was quite voluminous and presented a singular array of reasons why it would be impossible for him to meet Mr. Lincoln according to the terms of the challenge. His chief objection was that [his party's slate]—the Democratic candidates for Congress and the legislature—desired to address the people at the various county seats in conjunction with him; a pretext which, whether true or not as to the "desire," was found to be altogether untrue as to the fulfillment.

---

[1]   Norman B. Judd (1815-78) was an official of Mr. Lincoln's Republican Party.

Mr. Douglas, nevertheless, consented to seven meetings with his opponent for joint discussion; to wit, at Ottawa, Freeport, Jonesboro, Charleston, Galesburg, Quincy, and Alton. Mr. Lincoln, of course, promptly acceded to this arrangement. As he could not prevail upon Douglas to meet him in discussion in every part of the State, he was willing to do the next best thing—meet him wherever he could have the opportunity.

[Editor's Note: With only a few exceptions, Mr. Douglas is averse to campaigning in northern Illinois, e.g., urban Chicago, where many voters are antislavery. Despite his own shifting views, his Democratic Party is still allied with the slave South. As such, the senator agrees to debate mostly in areas of divided or openly proslavery views in central and southern Illinois. Many recent settlers from nearby slave States reside in these downstate locales.]

[Yet, even before the debates, Mr. Lincoln politically damaged his opponent], Mr. Douglas having taken no notice at Chicago, Bloomington, or Springfield (where he made preliminary speeches) of the "conspiracy" to which his attention had been called by Mr. Lincoln in his speech of June 16. The latter [Lincoln] deemed it proper to take a default on him [i.e., by not commenting, Mr. Douglas admits a conspiracy to spread slavery]. And [Lincoln sought] to dwell somewhat upon the enormity of his [Douglas] having "left a niche in the Nebraska bill to receive the *Dred Scott* decision," which declared that a territorial legislature could not abolish slavery.

Mr. Douglas was not slow in discovering that this charge [Lincoln's accusation of conspiracy], fortified as it was by overwhelming evidence, had begun to *hurt*. Therefore, at Clinton, De Witt County, he [Douglas] took occasion to read the charge to his audience, and to say in reply that "his self-respect alone prevented him from calling it a falsehood." A few days later, the "self-respect" broke down, and at Beardstown, Cass County, he pronounced it, with much vehemence of gesture, "an infamous lie!"

Mr. Lincoln commenced his canvass of the State at Beardstown [in central Illinois], a place of considerable importance on the Illinois River, on the twelfth of August [1858]. At the conclusion of his speech on this occasion, he reviewed the conspiracy charge in a manner so forcible that it can only be told in his own language:

[Mr. Lincoln Accuses Mr. Douglas]

"I say to you, gentlemen, that it would be more to the purpose for Judge Douglas to say that he did *not* repeal the Missouri Compromise; that he did *not* make slavery possible where it was impossible before; that he did *not* leave a niche in the Nebraska bill for the *Dred Scott* decision to rest in; that he did *not* vote down a clause giving the people the right to exclude slavery if they wanted to; that he did *not* refuse to give his individual opinion whether a territorial legislature could exclude slavery; that he did *not* make a report to the Senate in which he said that the rights of the people in this regard were 'held in abeyance' and could not be immediately exercised; that he did *not* make a hasty endorsement of the *Dred Scott* decision over at Springfield; that he does *not* now endorse that decision; that *that*[1] decision does *not* take away from the territorial legislature the power to exclude slavery; and that he did *not* in the original Nebraska bill so couple the words *State* and *Territory* together —that what the Supreme Court has done in forcing open all the Territories for slavery, it may yet do in forcing open all the States—I say it would be vastly more to the point for Judge Douglas to say he did *not* do some of these things, did *not* forge some of these links of overwhelming testimony, than to go to vociferating about the country that possibly he may be obliged to hint that somebody is a liar!"

From Beardstown, Mr. Lincoln went up the Illinois River to Havana and Bath, Mason County; Lewistown and Canton, Fulton County; Peoria, Henry, Marshall County; speaking at each place, and thence to Ottawa on the twenty-first of August [1858], where the first joint debate was appointed to take place. An immense audience, estimated by the friends of both parties at about twelve thousand, had congregated to witness the first grand passage-at-arms.

---

[1] *That that* emerges as a powerful idiom of Mr. Lincoln's. In this restored edition, emphasis is added to the second *that*.

The Lost Statesman

Stephen Douglas (1813-61) and Abraham Lincoln were rivals for most of their adult lives. What began as a squabble among penniless

youths, ended as a Shakespearean tragedy among statesmen. For decades, they battled for fame and fortune, climaxing only on the threshold of the presidency. They competed as lawyers, legislators, and even as eager suitors for the young socialite Mary Todd. (She married Mr. Lincoln.)

However, in the beginning, it was the brash Stephen Douglas who seemed destined for glory. As late as 1859, Mr. Douglas basked in the limelight, while the struggling Mr. Lincoln was without political prospects.

Some thought Stephen Douglas might yet be the great statesman who could unify the nation. The "Little Giant," though, possessed a moral blind spot: He prospered politically by ignoring the brutality of slavery.

Blind Spot
Shackled Slave

In 1854, as a powerful U.S. senator, Mr. Douglas ended the peaceful division of the American West into free and slave regions. To the cheers of slaveholders, he substituted "popular sovereignty," allowing voters to create slavery in areas Congress had reserved for a free society. Buoyed by the slave South, Mr. Douglas's presidential hopes rose.

Alas, a no-holds-barred contest at the ballot box mushroomed into the Civil War. Stephen Douglas failed to survive it. On June 3, 1861, only seven months after Abraham Lincoln defeated him for the presidency, Mr. Douglas, age 48, died of an exhaustion-related illness.

Before his death, he met and reconciled with Mr. Lincoln. Senator Douglas publicly pledged support to the new president and denounced the proslavery Confederacy that sought to break up the United States.

Library of Congress

Stephen Douglas, 1860

As a presidential candidate, he barnstormed the nation by overnight train. His health never fully recovered.

The Lincoln-Douglas Debates

Modern presidential debates descend from the debates of 1858 between Abraham Lincoln and Stephen Douglas. Slavery was the main issue, and the candidates' Senate race in 1858 was a dress rehearsal for their campaign for the presidency in 1860, two years later

However, neither man dominated the debates of 1858. Mr. Douglas was stronger initially, Mr. Lincoln better later. Nevertheless, as the challenger, Abraham Lincoln gained the most. Senator Douglas was already one of the most well-known politicians in America. Mr. Lincoln earned priceless name recognition simply by appearing on the same stage. To press his gains, the antislavery candidate compiled transcripts of the debates into a bestselling book that, like this biography, was an integral part of his presidential campaign.

[First Debate: Ottawa, Illinois]

Mr. Douglas had appointed to himself the opening and closing of the first and last of the seven discussions. Accordingly he occupied an hour in opening at Ottawa [on August 21, 1858], giving Mr. Lincoln an hour and a half to reply, and himself half an hour for rejoinder. The only thing of even moderate consequence presented in Mr. Douglas's first hour was a series of questions to his antagonist drawn from a series of radical antislavery resolutions which he alleged had been reported by Mr. Lincoln, as chairman of a committee, to the Republican State Convention of Illinois held at Springfield in October 1854.

To this Mr. Lincoln merely replied that no Republican State Convention was held at Springfield or anywhere else in 1854, and that he was not present at the *meeting* held there by a small number of persons, who nominated a candidate for state treasurer; on the contrary, he [Lincoln] was in another county, attending court.

Having disposed of this matter for the present, he [Lincoln] proceeded to occupy his time with the vital issues of the campaign, dwelling chiefly on the *Dred Scott* decision, and the peculiar reasons put forth by Mr. Douglas for sustaining it. "This man," said he [Lincoln, referring to Douglas], "sticks to a decision which forbids the people of a Territory from excluding slavery; and he does so not because he says it is right in itself—he does not give any opinion on that—but because it has been *decided by the court;* and being decided by the court, he is, and you are, bound to take it in your political action as *law*—not that he judges at all of its merits, but because a decision of the court is to him a *'Thus saith the Lord.'*[1]

"He [Douglas] places it on that ground alone, and you will bear in mind that this committing himself unreservedly to this decision, *commits him to the next one* just as firmly as to this. He did not commit himself on account of the merit or demerit of the decision, but it is a *Thus saith the Lord*. The next decision, as much as this, will be a *Thus saith the Lord*." *[Applause.]*[2]

Yet, as Mr. Lincoln proceeded to show, Mr. Douglas's public record presented three glaring instances of violation of Supreme Court decisions: (1) his repeated endorsement of General Jackson's course [a reference to President Andrew Jackson] in disregarding the decision of the Supreme Court declaring a national bank constitutional [in 1832]; (2) his endorsement of the Cincinnati platform [the 1856 policies of Mr. Douglas's Democratic Party], which says that Congress *cannot* charter a national bank, in the teeth of the Supreme Court decision declaring that Congress *can* do so; [and] (3) his notorious war upon the Supreme Court of Illinois which had decided that the governor could not remove a secretary of state, which ended in the appointment of five new judges, *of whom Douglas was one*, to vote down the four old ones. And here exactly was the time and place where Mr. Douglas acquired his title of "Judge!"

"These things," continued Mr. Lincoln, "show there is a purpose, *strong as death and eternity*, for which he adheres to this decision [*Dred Scott*], and for which he will adhere to *all other decisions* of the same court." *[Vociferous applause.]*

---

[1] A commandment that cannot be questioned, akin to the Word of God.

[2] These are restored crowd noises. Mr. Lincoln originally deleted them from debate transcripts. A complete record is in Edwin Erle Sparks, *The Lincoln-Douglas Debates of 1858* (Springfield: Illinois State Historical Society, 1908).

Debater
August 26, 1858

Gaunt and darkened by summer sun,
Mr. Lincoln sat for this portrait five
days after his first open-air debate with
Stephen Douglas on August 21, 1858.

Library of Congress

The following eloquent paragraph concluded the Ottawa debate
on Mr. Lincoln's part:—

[Slavery versus Liberty]

"Now, having spoken of the *Dred Scott* decision, one more
word, and I am done. Henry Clay [the former leader of the
Whig Party]—my *beau ideal* of a statesman, the man for whom
I fought all my humble life—Henry Clay once said of a class of
men who would repress all tendencies to liberty and ultimate
emancipation, that they must, if they would do this, go back to
the era of our independence, and muzzle the cannon which
thunders its annual joyous return; they must blow out the
moral lights around us; they must penetrate the human soul,
and eradicate there the love of liberty; and then, and not till
then, could they perpetuate slavery in this country! *[Loud cheers.]*

"To my thinking, Judge Douglas is, by his example and vast
influence, doing that very thing in this community *[cheers]*,
when he says that the Negro has nothing in the Declaration of
Independence. Henry Clay plainly understood the contrary.
Judge Douglas is going back to the epoch of our Revolution,
and, to the extent of his ability, muzzling the cannon which
thunders its annual joyous return.

The Forgotten Peacemaker

Abraham Lincoln often praised Henry Clay (1777-1852), a former congressman from his birth State of Kentucky. Indeed, Henry

Clay, not Abraham Lincoln, might have been the great icon of American history

Henry Clay's moniker was the Great Compromiser, which, when bestowed in 1820, was high praise. Mr. Clay, then Speaker of the U.S. House of Representatives, miraculously brokered the Missouri Compromise, which peacefully shared the American continent between pro- and antislavery regions.

Henry Clay

As a result, the nation's bitter dispute over slavery subsided. The Missouri Compromise kept the peace for decades. Henry Clay also dreamed of unifying America with economic development. Modernization would supposedly make slavery financially unattractive, leading to its voluntary end.

The young Abraham Lincoln and his generation of reformers fervently embraced Mr. Clay's vision of nonviolent compromise. Even as late as April 1861, when proslavery rebels mobilized for war, the newly elected President Lincoln still sought reconciliation and accommodation, à la Henry Clay.

However, a militant generation of slaveholders rejected compromise. Their reply to President Lincoln was to fire upon surrounded federal troops at Fort Sumter, South Carolina. Henry Clay's dream ended. The nightmare of civil war began.

Image courtesy of Library of Congress.

[Mr. Lincoln at Ottawa, continued]

"When he [Douglas] invites any people willing to have slavery to establish it, he is blowing out the moral lights around us. [Cheers.] When he says, he 'cares not whether slavery is voted down or voted up'—that it is a sacred right of self-government —he is, in my judgment, penetrating the human soul, and eradicating the light of reason and the love of liberty in this American people. [Enthusiastic and continued applause.]

"And now I will only say that when, by all these means and appliances, Judge Douglas shall succeed in bringing public sentiment to an exact accordance with his own views—when these vast assemblages shall echo back all these sentiments—when they shall come to repeat his views and to avow his principles, and to say all that he says on these mighty questions—then it needs only the formality of the second *Dred Scott* decision [to force slavery into Free States]—which he endorses in advance— to make slavery alike lawful in all the States, old as well as new, North as well as South."

When Mr. Douglas had occupied his half hour, and the debate was finished, Mr. Lincoln was borne away from the stand on the shoulders of his friends, in a frenzy of enthusiasm.

[Freeport Debate]

Directly after the Ottawa debate, it was discovered that the resolutions which Mr. Douglas produced there, and declared to have been written by Mr. Lincoln at Springfield in 1854, were never adopted at that place by *anybody*, but had been passed by a local convention at Aurora, Kane County. Common people very naturally called it a forgery. At the Freeport debate, six days later [August 27], Mr. Lincoln referred to it in the following crushing paragraph:

[That Evil Genius]

"I allude to this extraordinary matter in this canvass. For some further purpose than anything yet advanced, Judge Douglas did not make his statement upon that occasion as of matters that he believed to be true—but he stated them roundly as *being true*, in such form as to pledge his veracity for their truth.

"When the whole matter turns out as it does, and when we consider who Judge Douglas is—that he is a distinguished senator of the United States—that he has served nearly twelve years as such—that his character is not at all limited as an ordinary senator of the United States, but that his name has become of worldwide renown—it is *most extraordinary* that he should so far forget all the suggestions of justice to an adversary, or of prudence to himself, as to venture upon the assertion of that which the slightest investigation would have shown him to be wholly false. *[Cheers.]*

"I can only account for his having done so upon the supposition that *that* evil genius which has attended him through his life, giving to him an astonishing prosperity—such as to lead very many good men to doubt there being any advantage in virtue over vice *[cheers and laughter]*—I say, I can only account for it on the supposition that *that* evil genius has at last made up its mind to forsake him." *[Continued cheers and laughter.]*

The questions propounded by Mr. Douglas to his antagonist at Ottawa were still outstanding, unanswered. At Freeport, Mr. Lincoln took them up, and replied to them *seriatim*, as follows:

[Mr. Douglas's Questions, Mr. Lincoln's Answers]

Question 1. "I [Douglas] desire to know whether Lincoln today stands pledged, as he did in 1854, in favor of the unconditional repeal of the Fugitive Slave law?"

Answer. "I [Lincoln] do not now, nor ever did, stand pledged in favor of the unconditional repeal of the Fugitive Slave law." *[Cries of of 'Good! good!']*

Q. 2. "I desire him to answer whether he stands pledged today, as he did in 1854, against the admission of any more slave States into the Union, even if the people want them?"

A. "I do not now, nor ever did, stand pledged against the admission of any more slave States into the Union."[1]

---

[1] However, Mr. Lincoln opposes slavery in new *Territories,* from which new *States* emerge. This makes new slave *States* unlikely, although not impossible.

Library of Congress

Black Americans Hunted, 1850

In 1850, U.S. Senator Stephen Douglas cosponsored the Fugitive Slave Act, giving government officials the power to detain any person as an escaped slave. Abuses followed, e.g., falsely accusing and selling free blacks into slavery. Seeking nonviolent compromise, Mr. Lincoln in 1858 only suggested reform, not repeal. Some antislavery activists took umbrage. By 1860, though, looming civil war overshadowed the issue. Most antislavery voters drifted back to Mr. Lincoln.

[Douglas's Questions & Lincoln's Answers, continued:]

Q. 3. "I [Douglas] want to know whether he stands pledged against the admission of a new State into the Union with such a Constitution as the people of that State may see fit to make?"

A. "I [Lincoln] do not stand pledged against the admission of a new State into the Union, with such a Constitution as the people of that State may see fit to make." *[Cries of "Good! good!"]*

Q. 4. "I want to know whether he stands today pledged to the abolition of slavery in the District of Columbia?"

A. "I do not stand today pledged to the abolition of slavery in the District of Columbia."

Q. 5. "I desire him to answer whether he stands pledged to the prohibition of the slave trade between the different States?"

A. "I do not stand pledged to the prohibition of the slave trade between the different States."

Q. 6. "I [Douglas] desire to know whether he stands pledged to prohibit slavery in all the Territories of the United States, North as well as South of the Missouri Compromise line?"

A. "I [Lincoln] am impliedly, if not expressly, pledged to a belief in the *right* and *duty* of Congress to prohibit slavery in all the United States Territories [the new frontier lands of the American West]." *[Great applause.]*

Q. 7. "I desire him to answer whether he is opposed to the acquisition of any new territory unless slavery is first prohibited therein?"

A. "I am not generally opposed to honest acquisition of territory; and, in any given case, I would or would not oppose such acquisition, according as I might think such acquisition, would or would not aggravate the slavery question among ourselves. *[Cries of 'Good! good!']*

[Mr. Lincoln Elaborates]

"Now, my friends, it will be perceived, upon an examination of these questions and answers, that so far I have only answered that I was not *pledged* to this, that, or the other. The Judge has not framed his interrogatories to ask me anything more than this, and I have answered in strict accordance with the interrogatories, and have answered truly that I am not *pledged* at all upon any of the points to which I have answered. But I am not disposed to hang upon the exact form of his interrogatory. I am rather disposed to take up at least some of these questions, and state what I really think upon them.

"As to the first one, in regard to the Fugitive Slave law, I have never hesitated to say, and I do not now hesitate to say, that I think, under the Constitution of the United States, the people of the Southern States are entitled to a Congressional Fugitive Slave law. Having said that, I have had nothing to say in regard to the existing Fugitive Slave law, further than that I think it should have been framed so as to be free from some of the objections that pertain to it, without lessening its efficiency. And inasmuch as we are not now in an agitation in regard to an alteration or modification of that law, I would not be the man to introduce it as a new subject of agitation, upon the general question of slavery.

"In regard to the other question, of whether I am pledged to the admission of any more slave States into the Union, I state to you very frankly that I would be exceedingly sorry ever to be put in a position of having to pass upon that question. I should be exceedingly glad to know that there would never be another slave State admitted into the Union *[applause]*; but I must add that if slavery shall be kept out of the Territories during the territorial existence of any one given Territory, and then the people shall, having a fair chance and a clear field when they come to adopt the Constitution, do such an extraordinary thing as to adopt a slave Constitution, uninfluenced by the actual presence of the institution among them, I see no alternative, if we own the country, but to admit them into the Union. *[Applause.]*

"The third interrogatory is answered by the answer to the second, it being, as I conceive, the same as the second.

"The fourth one is in regard to the abolition of slavery in the District of Columbia. In relation to that, I have my mind very distinctly made up. I should be exceedingly glad to see slavery abolished in the District of Columbia. *[Cries of of 'Good! good!']* I believe that Congress possesses the Constitutional power to abolish it.

"Yet, as a member of Congress, I should not, with my present views, be in favor of endeavoring to abolish slavery in the District of Columbia, unless it would lie upon these conditions: *First,* that the abolition should be gradual; *second,* that it should be on a vote of the majority of qualified voters in the District; and *third*, that compensation should be made to unwilling owners. With these three conditions, I confess I would be exceedingly glad to see Congress abolish slavery in the District of Columbia, and in the language of Henry Clay, 'sweep from our Capital that foul blot upon our nation.'" *[Loud applause.]*

"In regard to the fifth interrogatory, I must say here, that as to the question of the abolition of the slave trade between the different States, I can truly answer, as I have, that I am *pledged* to nothing about it. It is a subject to which I have not given that mature consideration that would make me feel authorized to state a position so as to hold myself entirely bound by it.

"In other words, that question has never been prominently enough before me to induce me to investigate whether we really have the constitutional power to do it. I could investigate it, if I had sufficient time, to bring myself to a conclusion upon that subject; but I have not done so, and I say so frankly to you here, and to Judge Douglas.

"I must say, however, that if I should be of opinion that Congress does possess the constitutional power to abolish the slave trade among the different States, I should still not be in favor of the exercise of that power, unless upon some conservative principle, as I conceive it, akin to what I have said in relation to the abolition of slavery in the District of Columbia.

"My answer as to whether I desire that slavery should be prohibited in all the Territories of the United States, is full and explicit within itself, and cannot be made clearer by any comments of mine. So I suppose in regard to the question whether I am opposed to the acquisition of any more territory unless

Enigma
Summer 1858

A ghostly Abraham Lincoln appears in a white linen suit.

Tarbell, 1896

slavery is first prohibited therein, my answer is such that I could add nothing by way of illustration, or making myself better understood, than the answer which I have placed in writing."

Mr. Lincoln having answered all the questions propounded by his adversary, as Senator Benjamin [D-La.] observes,[1] "with no equivocation, no evasion," it now became his turn to interrogate. The two prominent facts of the campaign, in Mr. Lincoln's view, were "popular sovereignty" so-called; and the *Dred Scott* decision —each a sham and a fraud, yet directly antagonistic.

Mr. Lincoln therefore resolved to present them to Mr. Douglas in the form of a brief interrogatory, so worded that even the latter could find no avenue for escaping or dodging the contradiction.

[Stratagems]

[Editor's Note: Stephen Douglas claimed to support both "popular sovereignty" and *Dred Scott.* Mr. Lincoln sees a contradiction. Popular sovereignty empowered people in frontier Territories to locally decide the slavery issue. However, in *Dred Scott,* the Supreme Court curtailed local power. Settlers in the Territories could only vote *for* slavery, never against it. Hence, *Dred Scott* negated popular sovereignty; Mr. Douglas could not logically support both.

Mr. Lincoln responds slyly. He offers his foe a chance to correct his misstep in their Senate race, hoping Mr. Douglas will utter a further gaffe that will cripple a presidential bid in 1860. Mr. Lincoln plans to entice Mr. Douglas into repudiating *Dred Scott,* a proslavery policy deeply unpopular in Illinois. The opportunistic senator is likely to shift *against* slavery to gain local votes. If Mr. Douglas takes the bait, he inadvertently offends longtime supporters in slave States of the South.]

He [Lincoln] mentioned to some of his friends at Freeport that such was his purpose. They unanimously counseled him to let that topic alone; "For," said they, "if you put that question to him, he will perceive that an answer giving practical force and effect to the *Dred Scott* decision in the Territories, inevitably loses him the battle [in Illinois]; and he will therefore reply by affirming the decision as an abstract principle, but denying its practical application." [I.e., Mr. Douglas will claim *Dred Scott* does *not* expand slavery.]

---

[1]   U.S. Senator Judah P. Benjamin (1811-84) was proslavery, but in May 1860, praised Mr. Lincoln's honesty. The gesture was a slap at fellow Democrat Stephen Douglas, for alleged betrayal of the slave South in the 1858 debates.

Roger Taney (1777-1864)
Chief Justice, 1836-64
U.S. Supreme Court

His Dred Scott *decision denied citizen-*
ship to black people and ended a ban on
slavery in new Territories of the West.

Library of Congress

"But," said Mr. Lincoln, "if he does that, he can never be president [because he alienates his Southern allies who favor *Dred Scott*]." His [Lincoln's] friends replied with one voice, "That's not your lookout; you are after the *senatorship.*"

"No, gentlemen," rejoined Mr. Lincoln, *"I am killing larger game.* The battle of 1860 is worth a hundred of this!"

So the questions were put, and Mr. Douglas was forced to avow his dogma of "unfriendly legislation." [Mr. Douglas hinted that voters and legislators in new Territories could tacitly negate the proslavery *Dred Scott* decision—which he still endorsed.] His [Douglas's] present position as the candidate for the presidency of a faction of his party [without its Southern wing] verifies Mr. Lincoln's prediction.

[Editor's Note: In the above dialog, Mr. Lincoln refers to the 1860 campaign for the presidency, but probably not for himself. He made the remarks in 1858 when U.S. Senator William Seward of New York led the antislavery movement. Rather, Mr. Lincoln helps their mutual cause by sabotaging the presidential hopes of Stephen Douglas, their perennial opponent.

As predicted, Mr. Douglas's reversal on *Dred Scott* angered allies in the slave South. They were already troubled by his unexpected opposition to a proslavery constitution for Kansas. In 1860, many Southerners withdrew from Mr. Douglas's Democratic Party, dooming his bid for the White House.

New technology contributed to Mr. Douglas's woes. In past years, his opportunistic shift on slavery might have been only a local matter; he made his comments in Freeport, a small rural town. In 1858, the telegraph transmitted his "Freeport Doctrine" nationally, making it a major campaign blunder.]

[Appeal to Conservatives]

The third joint discussion [of the Lincoln-Douglas debates] was held nineteen days later, at Jonesboro, Union County (Lower Egypt),[1] on the fifteenth of September [1858]. The intervening time was occupied by Mr. Lincoln in active canvassing [in both northern and southern Illinois]. He spoke successively to large audiences at Fremont, Carlinville, Clinton, Bloomington, Monticello, Mattoon, Paris, Hillsborough, Edwardsville, and Greenville.

At Edwardsville, Madison County, Mr. Lincoln had comparatively a small audience, three or four hundred, perhaps. [The area had many settlers from slave States.] This county was one of four in the State which gave a plurality for Mr. Fillmore in 1856 [in that year's three-way presidential election], the vote standing: Fillmore, 1,658; Buchanan, 1,451; Frémont, 1,111.

[Editor's Note: In 1856, Millard Fillmore was the presidential nominee of the Know-Nothing Party, an anti-immigrant splinter group. He and the Democratic candidate, James Buchanan, were allies of slaveholders. In Edwardsville, their combined vote in 1856 was nearly triple that of the antislavery Republican, John C. Frémont. Undaunted, Mr. Lincoln plows ahead with an antislavery speech. Violence was possible.]

Notwithstanding the "conservative" character of the people in this latitude [southern Illinois], Mr. Lincoln gave them a straightforward Republican speech, without altering or modifying a syllable of the party creed, concluding with the following masterly appeal to the reason and consciences of his hearers:

[Slavery Threatens All People]

"My friends, I have endeavored to show you the logical consequences of the *Dred Scott* decision, which holds that the people of a Territory [the frontier lands of the West] cannot prevent the establishment of slavery in their midst. I have stated what cannot be gainsaid, that the grounds upon which this decision is made are equally applicable to the Free States as to the Free Territories, and that the peculiar reasons put forth by Judge Douglas for endorsing this decision, commit him in ad-

---

[1] Nickname for southern Illinois, whose major city is Cairo.

Stephen Douglas
Autumn 1858?

The strong midday lighting of this un-
dated photograph is rare for the era.
The image may be from the Lincoln-
Douglas debates, which were outdoors.

Tarbell, 1907

vance to the next decision, and to all other decisions emanating from the same source.

"And when by all these means you have succeeded in dehumanizing the Negro; when you have put him down, and made it impossible for him to be but as the beasts of the field; when you have extinguished his soul, and placed him where the ray of hope is blown out—in the darkness that broods over the damned—are you quite sure the demon [slavery] you have roused will not turn and rend you?

"What constitutes the bulwark of our liberty and independence? It is not our frowning battlements, our bristling sea-coasts, the guns of our war steamers, or the strength of our gallant army. These are not our reliance against a resumption of tyranny in our land. All of them may be turned against our liberties, without making us stronger or weaker for the struggle.

"Our reliance [against tyranny] is in the love of liberty which God has planted in our bosoms. Our defense is in the preservation of the spirit which prizes liberty as the heritage of *all men, in all lands, everywhere.* Destroy this spirit, and you have planted the seeds of despotism around your own doors.

"Familiarize yourselves with the chains of bondage, and you are preparing your own limbs to wear them. [If you become] accustomed to trample on the rights of those around you, you have lost the genius of your own independence, and become the fit subjects of the first cunning tyrant who rises among you. And let me tell you that all these things are prepared for you with the logic of history—if the elections shall promise that the next *Dred Scott* decision, and all future decisions, will be quietly acquiesced in by the people."

[Jonesboro Debate]

After making a similar speech at Greenville, Bond County—whose presidential vote stood in 1856: Fillmore,[1] 659; Buchanan, 607; Frémont, 153 [eight to one for allies of slaveholders]; but which was nevertheless carried in 1858 by Mr. [Joseph] Gillespie, the Republican candidate for state senator—Mr. Lincoln proceeded to the Jonesboro "milk-pan," as he facetiously termed it, because Mr. Douglas had said at Ottawa, in his usual ornate style, that he was "going to trot him (Mr. L.) down to Egypt, and bring him to his milk."[2]

[Editor's Note: At Jonesboro on September 15, 1858, Mr. Lincoln further exploited his opponent's reversal of policy at Freeport on August 27, nineteen days earlier. At the August event, Stephen Douglas hinted that settlers in the Territories could enact "unfriendly legislation" to negate *Dred Scott,* a proslavery policy that he backed. This angered supporters of Mr. Douglas in slave States, but now Mr. Lincoln charged him with also misleading *antislavery* voters, i.e., they could *not* negate *Dred Scott.* Mr. Lincoln implied that his foe was merely an opportunist who shifted with the political winds.]

In this debate, Mr. Lincoln devoted considerable attention to the "unfriendly legislation" dodge, clearly demonstrating that if the Constitution confers the right of taking slaves into the Territories [as the Supreme Court declared in *Dred Scott*], the territorial legis-

---

[1]   Misspelled here as *Filmore* in the 1860 text. See Editor's Note, page 160.

[2]   A derogatory idiom.

lature cannot annul the right, and that Congress is bound to give the slaveholder ample protection in the enjoyment of that right, should the territorial legislature neglect to do so.

Subsequently in a speech at Columbus, Ohio, Mr. Lincoln gave the finishing blow to "unfriendly legislation" in the following terse and admirable definition:

> "[The Supreme Court declares that] the *Dred Scott* decision expressly gives every citizen of the United States a right to carry his slaves into the United States' Territories [the new lands of the American West]. And now there was some inconsistency in [Mr. Douglas] saying that the decision was right, and saying too that the people of the Territory could lawfully drive slavery out again. When all the trash, the words, the collateral matter, was cleared away from it—all the chaff was fanned out of it—it was a bare absurdity, *no less than that a thing may be lawfully driven away from where it had a lawful right to be.*"

[Charleston Debate]

The fourth joint discussion took place at Charleston, Coles County, on the eighteenth of September [1858], three days after the Jonesboro debate, Mr. Lincoln having the opening and closing. This debate was remarkable chiefly for the fact that Mr. Lincoln fastened upon his antagonist [Douglas], by incontrovertible proof, the charge of having conspired with Senator Toombs [D-Ga.][1] and others to bring Kansas into the Union,[2] without having her Constitution submitted to a vote of the people, *for the purpose of making her a slave State.* Whoever will turn to that debate and examine the proofs presented by Mr. Lincoln, cannot possibly entertain a doubt as to the existence of such a conspiracy, and that Douglas was a party to it.

---

[1]   The ominously named Robert A. Toombs (1810-85) of Georgia was ardently proslavery. He was a former Whig colleague of young Congressman Lincoln in the 1840s, but in the late 1850s switched to the proslavery Southern Democrats. In 1861, Mr. Toombs became secretary of state of the Confederate States, and fiercely advocated war with the new U.S. president, Abraham Lincoln.

[2]   *Union* is shorthand for the United States of America. See note, page 49.

[Reply to Race-Baiting]

"Negro equality," the peculiar bugaboo of Mr. Douglas, also received a few moments' attention from Mr. Lincoln at Charleston, in these words:

[Editor's Note: Attempting to distract voters from the slavery issue, Stephen Douglas stoked racial fears. He repeatedly accused Abraham Lincoln of advocating equality and marriage with so-called "inferior races." Prejudice was then widespread. Voters began to shift.

Mr. Lincoln replies at Charleston, Illinois, on September 18, 1858. He seems trapped. A restless audience of 12,000 people faces him; many are recent settlers from nearby slave States. Their attitudes are conflicted. Some fear slavery's threat to *themselves*, but are also biased against the black slaves. That disconnect is the crux of the election. Many threaten a backlash if Mr. Lincoln endorses civil rights. Yet, if he accepts racial bias, he offends progressive supporters. Mr. Douglas has indeed set a trap.

Mr. Lincoln starts to speak. He seems to bow to prejudice, and to discard antislavery principles. However, a surprise is in store for all.]

"While I was at the hotel today, an elderly gentleman called upon me to know whether I was really in favor of producing a perfect equality between the Negroes and white people. *[Great laughter.]* While I had not proposed to myself on this occasion to say much on that subject, yet as the question was asked me, I thought I would occupy perhaps five minutes in saying something in regard to it.

"I will say, then, that I am not, nor ever have been, in favor of bringing about in any way the social and political equality of the white and black races *[applause]*; that I am not nor ever have been in favor of making voters or jurors of Negroes, nor of qualifying them to hold office, nor to intermarry with white people; and I will say in addition to this, that there is a physical difference between the white and black races which I believe will forever forbid the two races living together on terms of social and political equality. And inasmuch as they cannot so live, while they do remain together there must be the position of superior and inferior, and I, as much as any other man, am in favor of having the superior position assigned to the white race.[1]

---

[1] Frederick Douglass, the ex-slave, reported that, in private, Mr. Lincoln was free of bias. His public bias had an element of posturing, e.g., at Charleston.

"[Yet] I say upon this occasion, I do not perceive that because the white man is to have the superior position, the Negro should be denied everything. I do not understand that because I do not want a Negro woman for a slave, I must necessarily want her for a wife. [*Cheers and laughter.*] My understanding is that I can just let her alone. I am now in my fiftieth year, and I certainly never have had a black woman for either a slave or a wife. So it seems to me quite possible for us to get along without making either slaves or wives of Negroes.

"I will add to this, that I have never seen, to my knowledge, a man, woman, or child, who was in favor of producing a perfect equality, social and political, between Negroes and white men. I recollect of but one distinguished instance that I ever heard of so frequently as to be entirely satisfied of its correctness—and that is the case of Judge Douglas's old friend, Colonel Richard M. Johnson [a U.S. vice president allegedly involved in sexual misconduct with three of his slaves].[1] [*Laughter and cheers.*]

[Editor's Note: The crowd jeers Stephen Douglas. The tables turn. A conservative audience disapproves of the race-baiting Mr. Douglas.

For journalists, clergy, and others had long alleged sexual abuse of black slaves by white masters. Mr. Lincoln now broaches the taboo and ties his foe to the sordid scandal. In June 1857, a year before their Senate contest, Mr. Lincoln already rebuked him for indifference: "Judge Douglas is delighted to have them [black women] decided to be slaves ... and thus left subject to the forced concubinage of their masters." Mr. Lincoln cited statistical evidence of thousands of mixed-raced children born into slavery. Would-be allies of slaveholders recoiled; wavering voters defected. Six months later, in December 1857, Mr. Douglas began his reelection campaign by rejecting the proslavery Lecompton plan. (See page 136.)

Below, Mr. Lincoln adds more lip service to prejudice, but with caustic sarcasm. He all but repudiates his own words, while further complicating Mr. Douglas's efforts to exploit racism. A political trap goes awry.]

---

[1]   Richard M. Johnson (1780-1850), D-Ky., was vice president, 1837-41. He and three of his female slaves were a controversy of the era. The first slave allegedly bore his children and served in his household. In 1839, a report reached President Martin Van Buren that a second slave spurned Mr. Johnson, and he sold her; and that a third slave was a sister of the second. Mark O. Hatfield, *Vice Presidents of the United States, 1793-1993* (Washington: GPO, 1997), pp. 121-31.

Newton, 1910

Fourth Debate: Charleston, Illinois
Lithograph portrays debate of September 18, 1858. Abraham Lincoln stands in white coat, about to spring a surprise on Stephen Douglas, hand on hip.

"I will also add to the remarks I have made, (for I am not going to enter at large upon this subject) that I have never had the least apprehension that I or my friends would marry Negroes if there was no law to keep them from it *[laughter];* but as Judge Douglas and his friends seem to be in great apprehension that they might, if there were no law to keep them from it *[roars of laughter],* I give him the most solemn pledge that I will to the very last, stand by the law of this State, which forbids the marrying of white people with Negroes. *[Continued laughter and applause.]*

"I will add one further word, which is this: That I do not understand that there is any place where an alteration of the social and political relations of the Negro and the white man can be made except in the state legislature—not in the Congress of the United States—and as I do not really apprehend the approach of any such thing myself, and as Judge Douglas seems to be in constant horror that some such danger is rapidly approaching, I propose, as the best means to prevent it, that the Judge be kept at home [in Illinois and not the U.S. Senate], and placed in the state legislature to fight the measure. *[Uproarious laughter and applause.]*

[Galesburg Debate]

At the Galesburg debate [fifth in the series], held on the seventh of October [1858], Mr. Lincoln uttered the remarkable prediction concerning his adversary which we now see realized, in answer to one of Mr. Douglas's tirades about "sectionalism." [Mr. Douglas accused Mr. Lincoln of creating conflict between different sections of the nation. Mr. Lincoln allegedly appealed only to the antislavery States of the North, thereby alienating slave States of the South. Mr. Lincoln replies below.]

[Mr. Lincoln Rebuffs Mr. Douglas on Sectionalism]

"I ask his attention also to the fact that, by the rule of nationality [that local doctrines cannot be preached in foreign places], he is himself fast becoming sectional. *[Great cheers and laughter.]* I ask his attention to the fact that his speeches would not go as current now south of the Ohio River [in the slaveholding States] as they have formerly gone there.[1] *[Loud cheers.]*

"I ask his attention to the fact that he felicitates himself to-day that all the Democrats of the Free States are agreeing with him, while he omits to tell us that the Democrats of any slave State agree with him. If he has not thought of this, I commend to his consideration the evidence in his own declaration on this day, of his becoming sectional too. *[Immense cheering.]* I see it rapidly approaching. Whatever may be the result of this ephemeral contest between Judge Douglas and myself, I see the day rapidly approaching when his pill of sectionalism, which he has been thrusting down the throats of Republicans for years past, will be crowded down his own throat." *[Tremendous applause.]*

---

[1] Mr. Douglas angered his former allies in the slave South, because he shifted his views to appeal to antislavery voters in Northern States, e.g., Illinois. See preceding debates at Freeport and Jonesboro.

Tarbell, 1907

Fifth Debate: Galesburg, Illinois

Artist's sketch, circa 1895, depicts events of October 7, 1858 at Knox College, with 20,000 onlookers. Abraham Lincoln is in the distance, beneath the college banner, arm raised, and tall upon the stage of history.

The sixth (Quincy) debate took place on the thirteenth of October [1858]. It was at this meeting that Mr. Lincoln made an argument to prove that the *Dred Scott* premise, as to the constitutional right to take slaves into the Territories [the new lands of the West] —if carried to its logical results—would establish the right to take and hold them in the Free States also. Subsequently, Mr. Douglas, in his *Harper Magazine* article [of 1859], appropriated this argument of Mr. Lincoln to his own use, without giving credit therefor [and modified it to be more favorable to Mr. Douglas.]

[Editor's Note: The Free States used their local laws, not federal law, to ban slavery. Mr. Lincoln warned that the Supreme Court would soon strike down those state bans, just as they had the federal ban in new Territories. This would legalize slavery in all existing States, regardless of local opposition.]

The reader who will take the trouble to examine the volume of these debates, will find that, while Mr. Lincoln made a new argument at each meeting, Mr. Douglas's portion of each debate was substantially a repetition of his first effort at Ottawa [August 21, 1858].

[Alton Debate]

Two days later, on the fifteenth of October [1858], the final encounter between the champions took place at Alton [a river town in southern Illinois where an antislavery activist was murdered].[1] This volume would be incomplete without the admirable summing up of the ISSUES OF THE CAMPAIGN there appropriately presented by Mr. Lincoln. Let no one fail to peruse it:

[Slavery Morally Wrong]

"I have stated upon former occasions, and I may as well state again, what I understand to be the real issue in this controversy between Judge Douglas and myself. On the point of my wanting to make war between the Free and the slave States, there has been no issue between us. So too, when he assumes that I am in favor of introducing a perfect social and political

---

[1] In 1837, a mob in Alton killed Rev. Elijah P. Lovejoy, a religious publisher who crusaded for abolition, i.e., ending slavery. The Illinois legislature previously defended slavery. As a young solon, Mr. Lincoln filed a protest and later befriended the victim's brother, Rev. Owen Lovejoy, also an abolitionist.

Rectitude
October 1, 1858

*Fifteen months before the presiden-
tial campaign of 1860, Mr. Lincoln
was already a striking orator of
matchless ability.*

Tarbell, 1907

equality between the white and black races. These are false issues upon which Judge Douglas has tried to force the controversy. There is no foundation in truth for the charge that I
maintain either of these propositions.

"The real issue in this controversy—the one pressing upon
every mind—is the sentiment on the part of one class that
looks upon the institution of slavery *as a wrong*, and of another
class that *does not* look upon it as a wrong.

"The sentiment that contemplates the institution of slavery
in this country as a wrong, is the sentiment of the Republican
Party [of mine]. It is the sentiment around which all their actions, all their arguments, circle—from which all their propositions radiate. They look upon it [slavery] as being a moral, social, and political wrong; and while they contemplate it as such,
they nevertheless have due regard for its actual existence among
us, and the difficulties of getting rid of it in any satisfactory
way, and to all the constitutional obligations thrown about it.

"Yet, having a due regard for these, they desire a policy in
regard to it that looks to its *[sic]* not creating any more danger.
They insist that it should, so far as may be [practical], *be treated* as a wrong, and one of the methods of treating it as a wrong
is to *make provision that it shall grow no larger. [Loud applause.]*

They also desire a policy that looks to a peaceful end of slavery at some time, as [the remedy for it] being wrong. These are the views they entertain in regard to it, as I understand them; and all their sentiments—all their arguments and propositions—are brought within this range.

"I have said, and I repeat it here, that if there be a man amongst us who does not think that the institution of slavery is wrong in any one of the aspects of which I have spoken, he is misplaced, and ought not to be with us. And if there be a man amongst us who is so impatient of it as a wrong as to disregard its actual presence among us, and the difficulty of getting rid of it suddenly in a satisfactory way, and to disregard the constitutional obligations thrown about it, that man is misplaced if he is on our platform. We disclaim sympathy with him in practical action; he is not placed properly with us.

"On this subject of treating it as a wrong, and limiting its spread, let me say a word. Has anything ever threatened the existence of this Union [the national survival of the United States], save and except[1] this very institution of slavery? What is it that we hold most dear amongst us? Our own liberty and prosperity. What has ever threatened our liberty and prosperity, save and except this institution of slavery?

"If this is true, how do you propose to improve the condition of things by enlarging slavery—by spreading it out and making it bigger? You may have a wen or cancer upon your person and not be able to cut it out lest you bleed to death; but surely [enlarging] it is no way to cure it—to engraft it and spread it over your whole body. That is no proper way of treating what you regard us a wrong.

"[Yet, regarding slavery] you see this peaceful way of dealing with it as a wrong—restricting the spread of it, and not allowing it to go into new countries [the frontier Territories of the American West] where it has not already existed. That is the

---

[1] *Save and except* is an idiom for *but only.* In 1858, many already worried about the future of the Union, i.e., the survival of the United States as a nation.

peaceful way, the old-fashioned way, the way in which the [Founding] Fathers themselves set us the example.

"On the other hand, I have said there is a sentiment which treats it [slavery] as *not* being wrong. That is the Democratic [Party] sentiment of this day [as led by Mr. Douglas]. I do not mean to say that every man who stands within that range positively asserts that it is right. That class will include all who positively assert that it is right, and all who, like Judge Douglas, treat it as indifferent, and do not say it is either right or wrong. These two classes of men fall within the general class of those who do not look upon it as a wrong.

[Hypocrisy]

"And if there be among you anybody who supposes that he, as a Democrat, can consider himself 'as much opposed to slavery as anybody,' I would like to reason with him. You never treat it as a wrong. What other thing that you consider as a wrong, do you deal with as you deal with that? Perhaps you *say* it is wrong, *but your leader never does, and you quarrel with anybody who says it is wrong.*

"Although you pretend to say so yourself, you can find no fit place to deal with it as a wrong. You must not say anything about it in the Free States, *because it is not here.* You must not say anything about it in the slave States, *because it* is *there.* You must not say anything about it in the pulpit [of the churches], because that is religion and has nothing to do with it. You must not say anything about it in politics, *because that will disturb the security of 'my place.' [Shouts of laughter and cheers.]*[1] There is no place to talk about it as being a wrong, although you say yourself it *is* a wrong.

"But finally, you will screw yourself up to the belief that if the people of the slave States should adopt a system of gradual emancipation on the slavery question, you would be in favor of

---

[1] Stephen Douglas repeatedly referred to Mr. Lincoln as the challenger "for my place" in the U.S. Senate. It was initially an innocent remark, but Mr. Douglas became increasingly defensive. Political posters lampooned his insecurity over "my place," giving Mr. Lincoln an opening for the above quip.

it. You say that is getting it in the right place, and you would be glad to see it succeed. But you are deceiving yourself.

"You all know that Frank Blair and Gratz Brown [two anti-slavery politicians] down there in St. Louis,[1] undertook to introduce that system in Missouri. They fought as valiantly as they could for the system of gradual emancipation which you pretend you would be glad to see succeed. Now I will bring you to the test. After a hard fight [to win political support for freeing slaves], they were beaten, and when the news came over here, you threw up your hats and hurrahed for Democracy. *[Great applause and laughter.][2]*

"More than that, take all the argument made in favor of the system you have proposed [to allow slavery to expand], and it carefully excludes the idea that there is anything wrong in the institution of slavery. The arguments to sustain that policy carefully exclude it.

"Even here today, you heard Judge Douglas quarrel with me because I uttered a wish that it might sometime come to an end. Although Henry Clay could say he wished every slave in the United States was in the country of his ancestors [Africa], I am denounced by those pretending to respect Henry Clay for uttering a wish that it might sometime, in some peaceful way, come to an end. The Democratic [Party] policy in regard to that institution will not tolerate the merest breath, the slightest hint, of the least degree of wrong about it.

"[For example] try it by some of Judge Douglas's arguments. He says he 'don't care whether it [slavery] is voted up or voted down' in the Territories.

"I do not care myself, in dealing with that expression. [But] whether it is intended to be expressive of his individual sentiments on the subject, or only of the national policy he desires to have established, it is alike valuable for my purpose. Any man can say that [he 'don't care'], who does not see anything

---

[1] The 1860 text omits "down there in St. Louis."

[2] Mr. Lincoln's sarcasm also refers to the nickname of the Democratic Party.

wrong in slavery. But no man can logically say it *who does see a wrong in it,*[1] because no man can logically say he don't care whether a wrong is voted up or voted down. He may say he don't care whether an indifferent thing is voted up or down, but he must logically have a choice between a right thing and a wrong thing."

[Mr. Lincoln then directed attention to Mr. Douglas, seated nearby on the speakers' stand:]

"*He* [Douglas] contends that whatever community wants slaves has a right to have them. So they have—if it is not a wrong. But if it is a wrong, he cannot say people have a right to do wrong.

"*He* says that upon the score of equality, slaves should be allowed to go into a new Territory, like other property. This is strictly logical if there is no difference between it and other property. If it and other property are equal, his argument is entirely logical. But if you insist that one is wrong, and the other right, there is no use to institute a comparison between right and wrong.

"You may turn over everything in the Democratic [Party] policy from beginning to end—whether in the shape it takes on the statute book; in the shape it takes in the *Dred Scott* decision; in the shape it takes in conversation; or the shape it takes in short, maxim-like arguments—it everywhere carefully excludes the idea that there is anything wrong in it.

"That is the real issue. That is the issue that will continue in this country when these poor tongues of Judge Douglas and myself shall be silent. It is the eternal struggle between these two principles—right and wrong—throughout the world. They are the two principles that have stood face to face from the beginning of time, and will ever continue to struggle.

"The one is the common right of humanity, and the other the divine right of kings. It is the same principle in whatever shape it develops itself. It is the same spirit that says, 'You work and

---

[1] Emphasis added here, and in next three paragraphs.

toil and earn bread, and I'll eat it.' *[Loud applause.]* No matter in what shape it comes, whether from the mouth of a king who seeks to bestride the people of his own nation, and live by the fruit of their labor; or from one race of men as an apology for enslaving another race—it is the same tyrannical principle.

"I was glad to express my gratitude at Quincy [to Mr. Douglas for admitting he accepted slavery *forever* in America], and I reexpress it here to Judge Douglas—*that he looks to no end of the institution of slavery.* That will help the people to see where the struggle really is. It will hereafter place with us [on this side of the debate], all men who really do wish the wrong may have an end.

"And whenever we can get rid of the fog which obscures the real question—when we can get Judge Douglas and his friends to avow a policy looking to its perpetuation—[to admit that they favor slavery forever]—we can get out from among them that class of men [who believe it is a wrong], and bring them to the side of those who treat it as a wrong. Then there will soon be an end of it, and that will be its 'ultimate extinction.'

"Whenever the issue can be distinctly made, and all extraneous matter thrown out, so that men can fairly see the real difference between the parties, this controversy will soon be settled, and it will be done peaceably too. There will be no war, no violence. It will be placed again [on a path to a natural end] where the wisest and best men of the world placed it [when they founded the United States].

"Brooks of South Carolina [a proslavery former congressman][1] once declared that when this Constitution was framed, its framers did not look to the institution [slavery] existing until this day. When he said this, I think he stated a fact that is fully borne out by the history of the times. But he also said they [the Founding Fathers of America] were better and wiser men than the men of these days; yet the men of these days had experi-

---

[1]   In 1856, U.S. Representative Preston S. Brooks (1819-57), D-S.C., assaulted and nearly killed antislavery Senator Charles Sumner (1811-74), R-Mass.

ence which they had not, and by the invention of the cotton-gin [which increased the profitability of slavery][1] it became a necessity in this country that slavery should be perpetual.

"I now say that, willingly or unwillingly, purposely or without purpose, Judge Douglas has been the most prominent instrument in changing the position of the institution of slavery—which the Fathers of the government expected to come to an end ere[2] this—*and putting it upon Brooks's cotton-gin basis [great applause]*—placing it where he openly confesses he has no desire there shall ever be an end of it." *[Renewed applause.]*

The canvass was now finished—a canvass in some respects the most remarkable ever witnessed in this country—and naught remained but for the people to record their verdict. Each of the speakers addressed public meetings up to the day of election. Mr. Lincoln made about sixty speeches during the canvass, traversing almost the entire State by nearly every conceivable mode of travel. He spoke usually from two to three hours, nearly always in the open air, and to audiences so large as to require great effort on his part to be heard distinctly by all.

During these arduous labors, he never once faltered, never exhibited signs of weariness, never failed to meet an appointment. He seemed to grow fresher and stronger as the campaign progressed. Exercise in the open air, travel, and the excitement incident to the canvass, were, in some respects, a return to the habits of his early life, and the effect was plainly visible upon his physical mien.[3] His voice grew clearer and stronger to the very last day; and at the close he was heavier by nearly twenty pounds than at the beginning of the canvass.

He exhibited powers of endurance that have rarely been equaled. The gallant manner in which he bore himself at his meetings with Douglas, and the transcendent ability which he displayed

---

[1] Invented in 1793, the cotton-gin was a machine that speeded processing of cotton fiber. The device increased demand for more slaves to grow more cotton.

[2] *Ere* is a quaint word for *before.*

[3] Printed as "physical *man"* in 1860, but *mien,* or appearance, seems intended.

The Missing Recession

Mr. Lincoln's campaign book has an odd omission: He fails to blame his opponents for a deep economic recession. The "Panic of 1857" began just before his 1858 Senate race, and unemployment remained high throughout his 1860 presidential bid. During this period, Mr. Douglas's Democrats held the White House, but did little.

However, the causes of the recession were complex, and possible remedies, e.g., government regulation, were controversial. As such, Mr. Lincoln focused on denouncing slavery. Nevertheless, the hardships of the recession made voters more receptive to his main point: Slavery threatened all people, not just black slaves.

---

on all occasions, more than satisfied his friends. His progress through the State had all the characteristics of a triumphal march. He was met by large deputations from every town which he entered, tendering him, on behalf of its citizens,[1] a cordial welcome to their hospitalities, and a warm place in their affections.

The subsequent publication of his debates with Douglas—precisely as they were reported by their respective friends [in verbatim transcripts], without a word of comment or explanation, and its general circulation as a Republican campaign document [supporting antislavery principles]—is the highest testimonial that could be offered to the genius, to the ability, to the broad and comprehensive views, and to the statesmanlike character of Mr. Lincoln.

[Editor's Note: The biographer, Mr. Scripps, seems unaware that Mr. Lincoln compiled the manuscript for the above book by saving debate transcripts from newspapers. Nevertheless, as an editor, Mr. Lincoln was mostly impartial. He deleted crowd noises, e.g., applause, cheers, but changed little else.]

The election took place on the third of November [1858]. The excitement which had wrought the State up to a tempest during the progress of the fight, culminated on this eventful day. (The whole number of votes cast for president in Illinois in 1856 was 238,981; the whole number cast for members of the legislature in 1858 was 251,148.)[2]

---

[1] The 1860 text is "*in* behalf of its citizens," a likely misprint.

[2] A later tally suggests an even larger vote in 1858. See footnote on page 180.

Disappointment
October 1859

Mr. Lincoln lost his hard-fought race for the U.S. Senate in 1858, adding to a decade of defeats. "I now sink out of view and shall be forgotten," he lamented.

Herndon, 1895

A drenching and chilling rain poured down all day in the northern part of the State, extending southward, with more or less discomfort to voters, so far as Vandalia. It did not, however, reach "Lower Egypt" [a nickname for southern Illinois, where many Douglas voters lived; better weather favored their turnout].

The result of the election is matter of history. Mr. Lincoln had a majority over Mr. Douglas in the popular vote of 4,085 [or a margin of 1.6 percent of 251,148 votes];[1] while by an unfair apportionment law, the latter [Douglas] had a small majority of the legislature, and was therefore reelected to the Senate. [Before amendment in 1913, the U.S. Constitution required state legislatures, not the popular vote, to select senators.]

A careful analysis of the official returns reveals the following facts [regarding legislative districts in Illinois]:

[Gerrymandering]

First: That according to the census of 1855, the 33 districts carried by the Democrats [supporting Mr. Douglas], and electing 40 members, contained 606,278 population; and the 25 districts carried by the Republicans [supporting Mr. Lincoln] and electing 35 members, contained 699,840 population, or 93,562 more than the districts carried by the Democrats.

---

[1] The gap and vote may be larger. Allen C. Guelzo, *Lincoln and Douglas: The Debates that Defined America* (New York: Simon & Schuster, 2008), pp. 281-86.

Second: That in a Democratic district, the ratio of representation was 15,156 inhabitants to a member, while in Republican districts, it required 19,910 inhabitants to a member.

Third: That the true ratio being 17,421 inhabitants to a member, had the legislature been elected on that basis, the Republican districts would have been entitled to FORTY members of the [state] House and *fourteen* [state] senators; and the Democrats to *thirty-five* members of the House and *eleven* senators—exactly reversing the number each side secured. Of course, this would have elected Lincoln by the same majority on [the] joint ballot that Douglas received. Had every citizen possessed an equal weight and voice in the choice of [U.S.] senator, Mr. Douglas would now be a private citizen, and Mr. Lincoln a member of the U.S. Senate. Mr. Douglas is a senator from Illinois through a palpable violation of the principles of popular sovereignty [which he himself espouses].

[Editor's Note: As suggested above, Abraham Lincoln was deeply frustrated by his loss in the Senate contest of 1858. His old rival, Stephen Douglas, squeaked through reelection, despite repeatedly shifting his position on slavery. Soon thereafter, Senator Douglas blithely began his much anticipated campaign to win the presidency in 1860. By contrast, a dejected Mr. Lincoln returned to private life, believing his political career at end.

However, unbeknown to the alleged loser, he had become a national celebrity. Few had ever so vigorously challenged Senator Douglas, then one of the most powerful politicians in America. Mr. Lincoln soon received speaking invitations. By early 1860, he headed East on a lecture tour. Rev. Henry Ward Beecher, a renown antislavery activist, brought him to New York City.

At the Cooper Union college on February 27, 1860, Mr. Lincoln dramatically warned that slavery was "an evil not to be extended," and that it could "overrun us here in these Free States." Morality and patriotic duty demanded a vote for the antislavery cause. The New York media cheered both speech and speaker. Overnight, Abraham Lincoln became a presidential contender.

Within three months, on May 18, 1860, he overtook the elder statesman of the antislavery movement, William Seward, and captured the Republican nomination for president. (Mr. Seward was a U.S. senator from New York, and its former governor.) A month later, Stephen Douglas won the Democratic Party's nod for the White House. The presidential election of November 1860 would feature an historic rematch: Lincoln versus Douglas.]

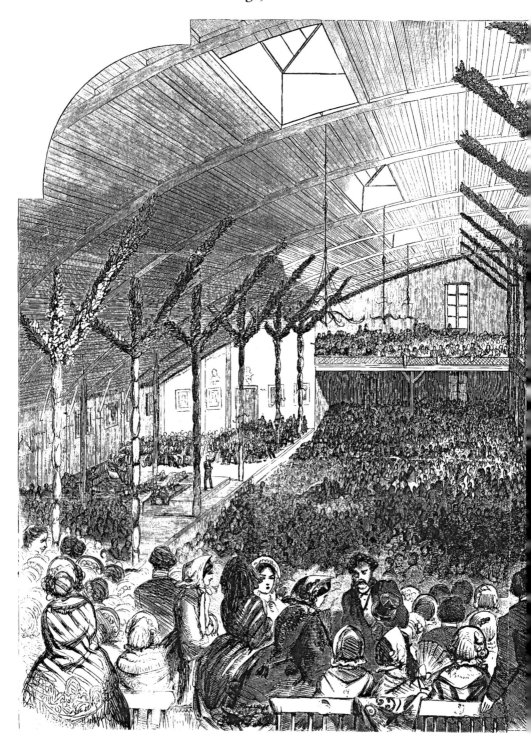

Below Facing Pages: Newspaper engraving depicts antislavery activists discussing presidential candidates at the 1860 Republican convention. Women were active and influential, even though barred from voting, or being official delegates. Many rallied to Mr. Lincoln. He publicly condemned sexual abuse of female slaves.

Mathew Brady, 1860/Stephenson, 1921

The Phoenix Rises
On February 27, 1860, Abraham Lincoln reprised his anti-slavery themes to a media audience at the Cooper Union, a new college in New York City. They cheered him. He believed the speech and this related photo made him president.

Conclusion

The man whose history we have thus briefly traced now stands before the country—the chosen candidate of the Republican Party for president of the United States. Commencing life under circumstances most discouraging,[1] we have seen him courageously and manfully battling his way upward from one position of honor and responsibility to another, until he now stands in an attitude to place his foot upon the very topmost round of honorable fame. He presents in his own person the best living illustration of the true dignity of labor, and of the genius of our free American institutions, having been elevated through their instrumentality from poverty and obscurity to his present distinguished position.

Perhaps no more appropriate conclusion can be given to this sketch of Mr. Lincoln's life than the following, relative to his personal appearance, habits, tastes, etc. (which is copied from the Chicago *Press and Tribune*, and for the correctness of which, in every particular, we can fully vouch):[2]

> "Mr. Lincoln stands six feet four inches high in his stockings. His frame is not muscular, but gaunt and wiry. In walking, his gait, though firm, is never brisk. He steps slowly and deliberately, almost always with his head inclined forward, and his hands clasped behind his back. In manner, he is remarkably cordial and, at the same time, simple. His politeness is always sincere, but never elaborate and oppressive. A warm shake of

---

[1] The 1860 text is "*the* most discouraging," either an error or outdated idiom.

[2] "*We can fully vouch*" refers to the newspaper's staff. This book's coauthor, Mr. Scripps, was a founder and editor of the paper. The quoted article was based on an exclusive interview Mr. Lincoln gave him.

the hand and a warmer smile of recognition are his methods of greeting his friends.

"At rest, his features, though they are those of a man of mark [or high stature], are not such as belong to a handsome man; but when his fine dark-gray eyes are lighted up by any emotion, and his features begin their play, he would be chosen from among a crowd as one who had in him not only the kindly sentiments which women love, but the heavier metal of which full-grown men and presidents are made. His hair is black and, though thin, is wiry.

"His head sits well on his shoulders, but beyond that, it defies description. It nearer resembles that of Clay than Webster's

SPRINGFIELD ILLINOIS

[From the Daily Journal of the 9th.]

WE ARE COMING!

CLEAR THE TRACK!

A Political Earthquake !

THE PRAIRIES ON FIRE FOR LINCOLN!

THE BIGGEST DEMONSTRATION EVER HELD IN THE WEST!

75,000 REPUBLICANS IN COUNCIL !

IMMENSE PROCESSION!

Speaking from Five Stands by Trumbull, Doolittle, Kellogg, Palmer, Browning, Gillespie, etc., etc.

MAGNIFICENT TORCHLIGHT PROCESSION AT NIGHT.

MEETINGS AT THE WIGWAM AND THE REPRESENTATIVES HALL.

August 1860/Oldroyd, 1896

[two former, well-regarded presidential candidates][1] but is unlike either. It is very large and phrenologically proportioned, betokening power in all its developments.[2] A slightly Roman nose and a wide-cut mouth and a dark complexion, with the appearance of having been weatherbeaten, complete the description.

"In his personal habits, Mr. Lincoln is as simple as a child. He loves a good dinner and eats with the appetite which goes with a great brain; but his food is plain and nutritious. He never drinks intoxicating liquors of any sort. He is not addicted to tobacco in any of its shapes. He was

---

[1]   Henry Clay and Daniel Webster were leaders and political moderates of Mr. Lincoln's first political party, the Whigs. The biographer, Mr. Scripps, is subtly comparing Mr. Lincoln to their longtime prominence in national affairs.

[2]   In the nineteenth-century, some believed that the shape of the head could reveal character traits of the person.

The Westerner
May 20, 1860

*Mr. Lincoln varied his public image.
With windswept hair, he appears here as
a homespun country lawyer—two days
after being nominated for president.*

Tarbell, 1907

never accused of a licentious act in his life. He never uses profane language. He never gambles. He is particularly cautious about incurring pecuniary obligations for any purpose whatever; and, in debt, he is never content until the score is discharged. We presume he owes no man a dollar.

"He never speculates [in the buying and selling of the public lands of the frontier]. The rage for the sudden acquisition of wealth never took hold of him.[1] His gains from his profession [as a lawyer] have been moderate, but sufficient for his purposes. While others have dreamed of gold, he has been in pursuit of knowledge.

"In all his dealings, he has the reputation of being generous but exact, and above all, religiously honest. He would be a bold man who would say that Abraham Lincoln ever wronged a man out of a cent, or ever spent a dollar that he had not honestly

---

[1] This is a veiled critique of Stephen Douglas, who, in 1856, raised eyebrows by reportedly netting $90,000 from land deals—over $2 million in modern dollars. He was already a U.S. senator and never worked in business. Mr. Lincoln joked about "evil genius," but nobody ever proved corruption. Henry Parker Willis, *Stephen A. Douglas* (Philadelphia: George W. Jacobs, 1910), pp. 145-46.

The Stay-at-Home Candidate

Abraham Lincoln's presidential campaign was historic in more ways than one. After being nominated for president in May 1860, he embarked on an unusual strategy to win the election that November: He stayed home. He never left small-town Springfield, Illinois. By contrast, his main rival for the presidency, Stephen Douglas, made a dramatic whistle-stop tour of the nation.

Even in his hometown, Mr. Lincoln avoided most public appearances. His self-imposed seclusion was born of both confidence and caution. As related in his book, Mr. Lincoln already hamstrung Stephen Douglas during their much-heralded debates in 1858, two years earlier. Goaded by Mr. Lincoln, his rival had carelessly alienated longtime supporters in the slave South.

Discretion, though, remained the better part of valor: Mr. Lincoln also feared making a gaffe. He led a fragile coalition of former opponents, Whigs and Democrats, against the expansion of slavery. He avoided jeopardizing this rare unity and quietly asked surrogates to campaign for their stay-at-home leader.

earned. His struggles in early life have made him careful of money, but his generosity with his own is proverbial.

"He is a regular attendant upon religious worship and, though not a communicant, is a pewholder and liberal supporter of the Presbyterian Church in Springfield, to which Mrs. Lincoln belongs. He is is a scrupulous teller of the truth—too exact in his notions to suit the atmosphere of Washington, as it now is. His enemies may say that he tells Black Republican lies; but no man ever charged that in a professional capacity, or as a citizen dealing with his neighbors, he would depart from the scriptural command [to do well unto others].

"At home, he lives like a gentleman of modest means and simple tastes. A good-sized house of wood, simply but tastefully furnished, surrounded by trees and flowers, is his own. There he lives, at peace with himself, the idol of his family; and

First Beard
November 25, 1860

Abraham Lincoln first sprouted his trademark beard after winning the presidential election. The stubble puzzled his aides and advisors.

Tarbell, 1907

for his honesty, ability, and patriotism, [he has] the admiration of his countrymen.

"If Mr. Lincoln is elected president, he will carry but little that is ornamental [or merely decorative] to the White House. The country must accept his sincerity, his ability, and his honesty, in the mold in which they are cast. He will not be able to make so polite a bow as Franklin Pierce [a wellborn president, who won the office in 1852, two elections earlier], but he will not commence anew the agitation of the slavery question by recommending to Congress any Kansas-Nebraska Bills.

"He [Lincoln] may not preside at the presidential dinners with the ease and grace which distinguish the "venerable public functionary," Mr. Buchanan [the incumbent president in 1860, and a former secretary of state]; but he will not create the necessity for a Covode Committee [a congressional investigation of alleged corruption][1] and the disgraceful revelations of Cornelius Wendell [a key witness against the Buchanan administration].

---

[1] Led by U.S. Representative John Covode (1808-71), R-Pa., one of the first antislavery Republicans elected to Congress.

The President-Elect Returns Home

Contemporary print supposedly depicts Abraham Lincoln returning on horseback after the presidential campaign. However, he never left his hometown of Springfield. On election night, he walked home from a local celebration.

"He [Lincoln] will take to the presidential chair just the qualities which the country now demands to save it from impending destruction—ability that no man can question; firmness that nothing can overbear; honesty that never has been impeached; and patriotism that never despairs."

- [End of 1860 text.] -

[Editor's Note: To foster unity among the antislavery Republicans, the book concludes without discussing Mr. Lincoln's stormy battle in early 1860 for the party's nomination for president. William Seward, his main rival for the nomination, never appears in the text. Instead, the book closes by directing its fire at the previous two U.S. presidents, Franklin Pierce and James Buchanan; both were allies of slaveholders.

In July 1860, Abraham Lincoln published his campaign biography in both Chicago and New York. The candidate largely avoided other substantive statements before that November's election. Even after winning, he declined to comment on major policy matters, e.g., the future of slavery, until after being inaugurated as president on March 4, 1861. (See following pages.)]

The Makeover of the President, 1861

In February 1861, shortly before embarking for Washington, D.C., President-elect Abraham Lincoln posed for this last publicity photo in his hometown of Springfield. His revamped image startled many. He had gained a beard, heft, styled hair, and elegant suits. (His wife, Mary, bought him a fresh wardrobe in New York City.)

His new beard, though, drew the most notice. No American president ever strutted facial hair in office. At the time, beards often had undesirable connotations, e.g., eccentricity. However, favorable notions also existed—wisdom, compassion, religiosity; the biblical figures of Christianity and Judaism all wore beards.

Mr. Lincoln never explained his beard, other than crediting a schoolgirl, Grace Bedell of New York State, for suggesting whiskers. Abraham Lincoln and his beard, though, would become American icons. (The next six U.S. presidents dutifully wore beards or mustaches.)

Presidential Inauguration of Abraham Lincoln
March 4, 1861

Above: Hatless and bearded, President-elect Lincoln enters capitol grounds in carriage with outgoing President James Buchanan (tipping hat).

Opposite page: Steps of U.S. Capitol during inauguration. Mr. Lincoln sits in the speakers' stand, partially behind post nearest to camera. The American flag salutes overhead; it waves in a steady breeze, creating a ghostly image.

Alexander Gardner, November 1863/Library of Congress

Quintessential Lincoln, 1863

A bearded sage replaced the novice of 1860. He repelled invasions by proslavery rebels; staved off foreign military intervention; and freed slaves. He appears here shortly before his Gettysburg Address, sanctifying Freedom as the sacred cause of the age.

New Epilogue

On November 6, 1860, Abraham Lincoln was elected president of the United States by winning the Free States of the North. His rival, Stephen Douglas, after years of shifting his position on slavery, lost in the Free North *and* slave South. (Third-party candidates John C. Breckinridge and John Bell swept the Southern States.)

However, by the time Abraham Lincoln was inaugurated as the sixteenth president on March 4, 1861, most slave States of the Deep South had withdrawn, or seceded, from the United States. The departing "Confederate States" condemned his election as "hostile to slavery," and their local militias mobilized for war.

In his inaugural address, President Lincoln appealed for reconciliation and offered to preserve the South's slavery in their home region. As promised by his campaign biography, the new president initially only forbade slavery's expansion into frontier Territories of the West.

Nevertheless, on April 12, 1861, Confederate rebels opened fire with heavy artillery on federal troops at Fort Sumter, South Carolina. Over 600,000 Americans lost their lives in the ensuing Civil War. President Lincoln and Congress gradually rescinded offers of compromise and supported abolition of *all* slavery.

The war ended in 1865, four years later. Federal armies repulsed slavery's threat, literally at the gates of Northern cities. However, within a few decades, ex-Confederate rebels violently deprived former slaves of civil rights in the Southern States. Some called it *de facto* slavery—slavery in all but name. (The federal government would not attempt to restore civil rights until a century after war's end.)

Among the war's final losses was Abraham Lincoln. He died on April 15, 1865, after being shot in Washington, D.C. A funeral train carried his coffin back to Springfield, Illinois. Millions of everyday Americans of all colors lined the train's route. President Lincoln had fought for their future as a free people; the people now honored him. His biography reached its final passage; he was going home.

New Appendix A

Abraham Lincoln's Autobiography
June 1860

[Editor's Note: In June 1860, Abraham Lincoln secretly and laboriously wrote in longhand his life story for use in this campaign biography. He is one of the few presidential candidates to do his own ghostwriting, anonymously describing himself in the *third* person.

His authorized biographer and coauthor, John Locke Scripps, disguised, polished, and integrated the candidate's manuscript into the much expanded full-length book.[1] At Mr. Lincoln's request, Mr. Scripps never mentions in the book the candidate's contribution. Even today, the general public is largely unaware that Abraham Lincoln wrote an autobiography, let alone one incorporated into a bestseller. (Mr. Scripps, though, reuses many phrases, helping historians identify the ghostwriter.)

Mr. Lincoln's original handwritten manuscript is now in the archives of the Library of Congress. This appendix reprints a contemporary transcription made by John Nicolay, a clerk in Mr. Lincoln's law office in Springfield. Mr. Nicolay was very familiar with his boss's handwriting and later became one of his secretaries in the White House.

Of particular interest are changes in tone in Mr. Lincoln's text. He describes his early personal life in a dry, almost clinical fashion. Then with great passion, he vigorously defends his political career, from its earliest days up to the presidential election of 1856. (Pressed for time, Mr. Lincoln never finished his manuscript. His biographer, Mr. Scripps, expanded and filled in the story up to 1860.)

What follows then is Abraham Lincoln's autobiography from his own hand, as transcribed in 1860, and then reprinted in 1894.[2] Also included is a related note given to a visiting portrait artist, Thomas Hicks of New York, on June 14, 1860. Minimal annotation is from the 1894 edition. Spelling, grammar, capitalization, etc., mirror the form of that reprint, e.g., the long paragraphs common to earlier centuries.]

---

[1]   Horace White, a reporter for the Chicago *Press & Tribune*, may have contributed material. In 1858, Mr. White covered the Lincoln-Douglas debates.

[2]   John G. Nicolay and John Hay, eds., *Abraham Lincoln: Complete Works*, 2 vol. (New York: The Century Company, 1894), I:638-644

June [1?], 1860.—SHORT AUTOBIOGRAPHY WRITTEN AT THE REQUEST OF A FRIEND TO USE IN PREPARING A POPULAR CAMPAIGN BIOGRAPHY IN THE ELECTION OF 1860.

Abraham Lincoln was born February 12, 1809, then in Hardin, now in the more recently formed county of La Rue, Kentucky. His father, Thomas, and grandfather, Abraham, were born in Rockingham County, Virginia, whither their ancestors had come from Berks County, Pennsylvania. His lineage has been traced no farther back than this. The family were originally Quakers, though in later times they have fallen away from the peculiar habits of that people. The grandfather, Abraham, had four brothers—Isaac, Jacob, John, and Thomas. So far as known, the descendants of Jacob and John are still in Virginia. Isaac went to a place near where Virginia, North Carolina, and Tennessee join; and his descendants are in that region. Thomas came to Kentucky, and after many years died there, whence his descendants went to Missouri. Abraham, grandfather of the subject of this sketch, came to Kentucky, and was killed by Indians about the year 1784. He left a widow, three sons, and two daughters. The eldest son, Mordecai, remained in Kentucky till late in life, when he removed to Hancock County, Illinois, where soon after he died, and where several of his descendants still remain. The second son, Josiah, removed at an early day to a place on Blue River, now within Hancock County, Indiana, but no recent information of or his family has been obtained. The eldest sister, Mary, married Ralph Crume, and some of her descendants are now known to be in Breckenridge County, Kentucky. The second sister, Nancy, married William Brumfield, and her family are not known to have left Kentucky, but there is no recent information from them. Thomas, the youngest son, and father of the present subject, by the early death of his father, and very narrow circumstances of his mother, even in childhood was a wandering laboring-boy, and grew up literally without education. He never did more in the way of writing than to bunglingly write his own name. Before he was grown he passed one year as a hired hand with his uncle Isaac on Watauga, a branch of the Holston River. Getting back into Kentucky, and having reached his twenty-eighth year, he married Nancy Hanks—mother of the present subject—in the year 1806. She also was born in Virginia; and relatives of hers of the name of Hanks, and of other names, now reside in Coles, in Macon, and in Adams Counties, Illinois, and also in Iowa. The present subject has no brother or sister of the whole or half blood. He had a sister, older than himself, who

was grown and married, but died many years ago, leaving no child; also a
brother, younger than himself, who died in infancy. Before leaving Kentucky, he and his sister were sent, for short periods, to A B C schools, the
first kept by Zachariah Riney, and the second by Caleb Hazel.

At this time his father resided on Knob Creek, on the road from Bards-
town, Kentucky, to Nashville, Tennessee, at a point three or three and a half
miles south or southwest of Atherton's Ferry, on the Rolling Fork. From this
place he removed to what is now Spencer County, Indiana, in the autumn
of 1816, Abraham then being in his eighth year. This removal was partly on
account of slavery, but chiefly on account of the difficulty in land titles in
Kentucky. He settled in an unbroken forest, and the clearing away of surplus wood was the great task ahead. Abraham, though very young, was
large of his age, and had an ax put into his hands at once; and from that till
within his twenty-third year he was almost constantly handling that most
useful instrument—less, of course, in plowing and harvesting seasons. At
this place Abraham took an early start as a hunter, which was never much
improved afterward. A few days before the completion of his eighth year, in
the absence of his father, a flock of wild turkeys approached the new log
cabin, and Abraham with a rifle-gun, standing inside, shot through a crack
and killed one of them. He has never since pulled a trigger on any larger
game. In the autumn of 1818 his mother died; and a year afterward his father married Mrs. Sally Johnston, at Elizabethtown, Kentucky, a widow
with three children of her first marriage. She proved a good and kind mother to Abraham, and is still living in Coles County, Illinois. There were no
children of this second marriage. His father's residence continued at the
same place in Indiana till 1830. While here Abraham went to A B C schools
by littles, kept successively by Andrew Crawford, —— Sweeney, and Azel
W. Dorsey. He does not remember any other. The family of Mr. Dorsey
now resides in Schuyler County, Illinois. Abraham now thinks that the aggregate of all his schooling did not amount to one year. He was never in a
college or academy as a student, and never inside of a college or academy
building till since he had a law license. What he has in the way of education
he has picked up. After he was twenty-three and had separated from his father, he studied English grammar—imperfectly, of course, but so as to
speak and write as well as he now does. He studied and nearly mastered
the six books of Euclid since he was a member of Congress. He regrets his
want of education, and does what he can to supply the want. In his tenth
year he was kicked by a horse, and apparently killed for a time. When he
was nineteen, still residing in Indiana, he made his first trip upon a flatboat

to New Orleans. He was a hired hand merely, and he and a son of the owner, without other assistance, made the trip. The nature of part of the "cargo-load," as it was called, made it necessary for them to linger and trade along the sugar-coast; and one night they were attacked by seven negroes with intent to kill and rob them. They were hurt some in the melee, but succeeded in driving the negroes from the boat, and then "cut cable," "weighed anchor," and left.

March 1, 1830, Abraham having just completed his twenty-first year, his father and family, with the families of the two daughters and sons-in-law of his stepmother, left the old homestead in Indiana and came to Illinois. Their mode of conveyance was wagons drawn by ox-teams, and Abraham drove one of the teams. They reached the county of Macon, and stopped there some time within the same month of March. His father and family settled a new place on the north side of the Sangamon River, at the junction of the timberland and prairie, about ten miles westerly from Decatur. Here they built a log cabin, into which they removed, and made sufficient of rails to fence ten acres of ground, fenced and broke the ground, and raised a crop of sown corn upon it the same year. These are or are supposed to be, the rails about which so much is being said just now, though these are far from being the first or only rails ever made by Abraham.

The sons-in-law were temporarily settled in other places in the county. In the autumn all hands were greatly afflicted with ague and fever, to which they had not been used, and by which they were greatly discouraged, so much so that they determined on leaving the county. They remained, however, through the succeeding winter, which was the winter of the very celebrated "deep snow" of Illinois. During that winter Abraham, together with his stepmother's son, John D. Johnston, and John Hanks, yet residing in Macon County, hired themselves to Denton Offutt to take a flatboat from Beardstown, Illinois, to New Orleans; and for that purpose were to join him —Offutt—at Springfield, Illinois, so soon as the snow should go off. When it did go off, which was about the first of March, 1831, the county was so flooded as to make traveling by land impracticable; to obviate which difficulty they purchased a large canoe, and came down the Sangamon River in it. This is the time and the manner of Abraham's first entrance into Sangamon County. They found Offutt at Springfield, but learned from him that he had failed in getting a boat at Beardstown. This led to their hiring themselves to him for twelve dollars per month each, and getting the timber out of the trees and building a boat at Old Sangamon town on the Sangamon

River, seven miles northwest of Springfield, which boat they took to New
Orleans, substantially upon the old contract.

During this boat-enterprise acquaintance with Offutt, who was previously an entire stranger, he conceived a liking for Abraham, and believing
he could turn him to account, he contracted with him to act as clerk for
him, on his return from New Orleans, in charge of a store and mill at New
Salem, then in Sangamon, now in Menard County. Hanks had not gone to
New Orleans, but having a family, and being likely to be detained from
home longer than at first expected, had turned back from St. Louis. He is
the same John Hanks who now engineers the "rail enterprise" at Decatur,
and is a first cousin to Abraham's mother. Abraham's father, with his own
family and others mentioned, had, in pursuance of their intention, removed
from Macon to Coles County. John D. Johnston, the stepmother's son, went
to them, and Abraham stopped indefinitely and for the first time, as it were,
by himself at New Salem, before mentioned. This was in July, 1831. Here
he rapidly made acquaintances and friends. In less than a year Offutt's
business was failing—had almost failed—when the Black Hawk war of
1832 broke out. Abraham joined a volunteer company, and, to his own surprise, was elected captain of it. He says he has not since had any success in
life which gave him so much satisfaction. He went to the campaign, served
near three months, met the ordinary hardships of such an expedition, but
was in no battle. He now owns, in Iowa, the land upon which his own warrants for the service were located. Returning from the campaign, and encouraged by his great popularity among his immediate neighbors, he the
same year ran for the legislature, and was beaten, —his own precinct, however, casting its votes 277 for and 7 against him—and that, too, while he
was an avowed Clay man, and the precinct the autumn afterward giving a
majority of 115 to General Jackson over Mr. Clay. This was the only time
Abraham was ever beaten on a direct vote of the people. He was now without means and out of business, but was anxious to remain with his friends
who had treated him with so much generosity, especially as he had nothing
elsewhere to go to. He studied what he should do—thought of learning the
blacksmith trade—thought of trying to study law—rather thought he could
not succeed at that without a better education. Before long, strangely
enough, a man offered to sell, and did sell, to Abraham and another as poor
as himself, an old stock of goods, upon credit. They opened as merchants;
and he says that was *the* store. Of course they did nothing but get deeper
and deeper in debt. He was appointed postmaster at New Salem—the office being too insignificant to make his politics an objection. The store

winked out. The surveyor of Sangamon offered to depute to Abraham that portion of his work which was within his part of the county. He accepted, procured a compass and chain, studied Flint and Gibson a little, and went at it. This procured bread, and kept soul and body together. The election of 1834 came, and he was then elected to the legislature by the highest vote cast for any candidate. Major John T. Stuart, then in full practice of the law, was also elected. During the canvass, in a private conversation he encouraged Abraham [to][1] study law. After the election he borrowed books of Stuart, took them home with him, and went at it in good earnest. He studied with nobody. He still mixed in the surveying to pay board and clothing bills. When the legislature met, the law-books were dropped, but were taken up again at the end of the session. He was reelected in 1836, 1838, and 1840. In the autumn of 1836 he obtained a law license, and on April 15, 1837, removed to Springfield, and commenced the practice—his old friend Stuart taking him into partnership. March 3, 1837, by a protest entered upon the "Illinois *House Journal*" of that date, at pages 817 and 818, Abraham with Dan Stone, another representative of Sangamon, briefly defined his position on the slavery question; and so far as it goes, it was then the same that it is now. The protest is as follows:

> Resolutions upon the subject of domestic slavery having passed both branches of the General Assembly at its present session, the undersigned hereby protest against the passage of the same.
>
> They believe that the institution of slavery is founded on both injustice and bad policy, but that the promulgation of Abolition doctrines tends rather to increase than abate its evils.
>
> They believe that the Congress of the United States has no power under the Constitution to interfere with the institution of slavery in the different States.
>
> They believe that the Congress of the United States has the power, under the Constitution, to abolish slavery in the District of Columbia, but that the power ought not to be exercised unless at the request of the people of the District.

---

[1]   Annotation from 1894 text.

The difference between these opinions and those contained in the above resolutions is their reason for entering
this protest.

DAN STONE,

A. LINCOLN,

Representatives from the County of Sangamon.

In 1838 and 1840, Mr. Lincoln's party voted for him as Speaker, but being in the minority he was not elected. After 1840 he declined a reelection to
the legislature. He was on the Harrison electoral ticket in 1840, and on that
of Clay in 1844, and spent much time and labor in both those canvasses. In
November, 1842, he was married to Mary, daughter of Robert S. Todd, of
Lexington, Kentucky. They have three living children, all sons, one born in
1843, one in 1850, and one in 1853. They lost one, who was born in 1846.

In 1846 he was elected to the lower House of Congress, and served one
term only, commencing in December, 1847, and ending with the inauguration of General Taylor, in March, 1849. All the battles of the Mexican war
had been fought before Mr. Lincoln took his seat in Congress, but the
American army was still in Mexico, and the treaty of peace was not fully
and formally ratified till the June afterward. Much has been said of his
course in Congress in regard to this war. A careful examination of the "Journal" and "Congressional Globe" shows that he voted for all the supply measures that came up, and for all the measures in any way favorable to the officers, soldiers, and their families, who conducted the war through; with the
exception that some of these measures passed without yeas and nays, leaving no record as to how particular men voted. The "Journal" and "Globe"
also show him voting that the war was unnecessarily and unconstitutionally
begun by the President of the United States. This is the language of Mr.
Ashmun's amendment, for which Mr. Lincoln and nearly or quite all other
Whigs of the House of Representatives voted.

Mr. Lincoln's reasons for the opinion expressed by this vote were briefly
that the President had sent General Taylor into an inhabited part of the
country belonging to Mexico, and not to the United States, and thereby had
provoked the first act of hostility, in fact the commencement of the war; that
the place, being the country bordering on the east bank of the Rio Grande,
was inhabited by native Mexicans, born there under the Mexican government, and had never submitted to, nor been conquered by, Texas or the
United States, nor transferred to either by treaty; that although Texas
claimed the Rio Grande as her boundary, Mexico had never recognized it,

and neither Texas nor the United States had ever enforced it; that there was a broad desert between that and the country over which Texas had actual control; that the country where hostilities commenced, having once belonged to Mexico, must remain so until it was somehow legally transferred, which had never been done.

Mr. Lincoln thought the act of sending an armed force among the Mexicans was unnecessary, inasmuch as Mexico was in no way molesting or menacing the United States or the people thereof; and that it was unconstitutional, because the power of levying war is vested in Congress, and not in the President. He thought the principal motive for the act was to divert public attention from the surrender of "Fifty-four, forty, or fight" to Great Britain, on the Oregon boundary question.

Mr. Lincoln was not a candidate for reelection. This was determined upon and declared before he went to Washington, in accordance, with an understanding among Whig friends, by which Colonel Hardin and Colonel Baker had each previously served a single term in this same district.

In 1848, during his term in Congress, he advocated General Taylor's nomination for the presidency, in opposition to all others, and also took an active part for his election after his nomination, speaking a few times in Maryland, near Washington, several times in Massachusetts, and canvassing quite fully his own district in Illinois, which was followed by a majority in the district of over 1500 for General Taylor.

Upon his return from Congress he went to the practice of the law with greater earnestness than ever before. In 1852 he was upon the Scott electoral ticket, and did something in the way of canvassing, but owing to the hopelessness of the cause in Illinois he did less than in previous presidential canvasses.

In 1854 his profession had almost superseded the thought of politics in his mind, when the repeal of the Missouri Compromise aroused him as he had never been before.

In the autumn of that year he took the stump with no broader practical aim or object than to secure, if possible, the reelection of Hon. Richard Yates to Congress. His speeches at once attracted a more marked attention than they had ever before done. As the canvass proceeded he was drawn to different parts of the State outside of Mr. Yates's district. He did not abandon the law, but gave his attention by turns to that and politics. The State agricultural fair was at Springfield that year, and Douglas was announced to speak there.

In the canvass of 1856 Mr. Lincoln made over fifty speeches, no one of which, so far as he remembers, was put in print. One of them was made at Galena, but Mr. Lincoln has no recollection of any part of it being printed; nor does he remember whether in that speech he said anything about a Supreme Court decision. He may have spoken upon that subject, and some of the newspapers may have reported him as saying what is now ascribed to him; but he thinks he could not have expressed himself as represented.

June 14, 1860. — AUTOBIOGRAPHICAL MEMORANDUM GIVEN TO THE ARTIST HICKS.

I was born February 12, 1809, in then Hardin County, Kentucky, at a point within the now county of La Rue, a mile, or a mile and a half, from where Hodgen's mill now is. My parents being dead, and my own memory not serving, I know no means of identifying the precise locality. It was on Nolin Creek.

June 14, 1860.   A. LINCOLN

New Appendix B
Antislavery Platform of the Republican Party, 1860

[Editor's Note: Abraham Lincoln campaigned on the widely distributed political platform of the antislavery Republican Party of 1860. Steadfastly honest, he adhered to the platform's policies after his election as president, making them a key part of his administration.

The platform banned slavery from new Territories of the American West; supported major transportation projects, then called "internal improvements"; granted government land to family farmers; and increased the tariff, or tax, on foreign products, to protect jobs and industries in the United States.

Also, as promised by Mr. Lincoln, the platform opposed federal efforts to immediately end slavery in existing States, believing the issue to be a "domestic" matter for States. The platform sought to limit, not abolish slavery.

What follows then is the platform of the Republican Party of 1860, as printed in Horace Greeley's *A Political Textbook for 1860* (New York: Tribune Association, 1860), pp. 26-27. Mr. Greeley was America's foremost publisher, and a sponsor of Mr. Lincoln's campaign biography.]

Resolved, That we, the delegated representatives of the Republican electors of the United States, in Convention assembled, in discharge of the duty we owe to our constituents and our country, unite in the following declarations:

1. That the history of the nation, during the last four years, has fully established the propriety and necessity of the organization and perpetuation of the Republican party, and that the causes which called it into existence are permanent in their nature, and now, more than ever before, demand its peaceful and constitutional triumph.

2. That the maintenance of the principles promulgated in the Declaration of Independence and embodied in the Federal Constitution, "That all men are created equal; that they are endowed by their Creator with certain inalienable rights; that among these are life, liberty and the pursuit of happiness; that, to secure these rights, governments are instituted among men, deriving their just powers from the consent of the governed," is essential to the preservation of our Republican institutions; and that the Federal Constitution, the Rights of the States, and the Union of the States, must and shall be preserved.

3.   That to the Union of the States this nation owes its unprecedented increase in population, its surprising development of material resources, its rapid augmentation of wealth, its happiness at home and
its honor abroad; and we hold in abhorrence all schemes for Disunion, come from whatever source they may: And we congratulate
the country that no Republican member of Congress has uttered or
countenanced the threats of Disunion so often made by Democratic
members, without rebuke and with applause from their political associates; and we denounce those threats of disunion, in case of a popular overthrow of their ascendency, as denying the vital principles of a
free government, and as an avowal of contemplated treason, which it
is the imperative duly of an indignant People sternly to rebuke and
forever silence.

4.   That the maintenance inviolate of the rights of the States, and especially the right of each State to order and control its own domestic
institutions according to its own judgment exclusively, is essential to
that balance of powers on which the perfection and endurance of our
political fabric depends; and we denounce the lawless invasion by
armed force of the soil of any State or Territory, no matter under what
pretext, as among the gravest of crimes.

5.   That the present Democratic Administration has far exceeded our
worst apprehensions, in its measureless subserviency to the exactions
of a sectional interest, as especially evinced in its desperate exertions
to force the infamous Lecompton Constitution upon the protesting
people of Kansas; in construing the personal relation between master
and servant to involve an unqualified property in persons; in its attempted enforcement, everywhere, on land and sea, through the intervention of Congress and of the Federal Courts of the extreme pre-
tensions of a purely local interest; and in its general and unvarying
abuse of the power intrusted to it by a confiding people.

6.   That the people justly view with alarm the reckless extravagance
which pervades every department of the Federal Government; that a
return to rigid economy and accountability is indispensable to arrest
the systematic plunder of the public treasury by favored partisans;
while the recent startling developments of frauds and corruptions at

the Federal metropolis, show that an entire change of administration is imperatively demanded.

7.   That the new dogma that the Constitution, of its own force, carries Slavery into any or all of the Territories of the United States, is a dangerous political heresy, at variance with the explicit provisions of that instrument itself, with contemporaneous[1] exposition, and with legislative and judicial precedent; is revolutionary in its tendency, and subversive of the peace and harmony of the country.

8.   That the normal condition of all the territory of the United States is that of freedom: That as our Republican fathers, when they had abolished Slavery in all our national territory, ordained that "no person should be deprived of life, liberty, or property, without due process of law," it becomes our duty, by legislation, whenever such legislation is necessary, to maintain this provision of the Constitution against all attempts to violate it; and we deny the authority of Congress, of a territorial legislature, or of any individuals, to give legal existence to Slavery in any Territory of the United States.

9.   That we brand the recent re-opening of the African slave-trade under the cover of our national flag, aided by perversions of judicial power, as a crime against humanity and a burning shame to our country and age; and we call upon Congress to take prompt and efficient measures for the total and final suppression of that execrabe traffic.

10.   That in the recent vetoes, by their Federal Government of the acts of the Legislatures of Kansas and Nebraska, prohibiting Slavery in those Territories, we find a practical illustration of the boasted Democratic principles of Non Intervention and Popular Sovereignty embodied in the Kansas-Nebraska bill, and a demonstration of the deception and fraud involved therein.

11.   That Kansas should, of right, be immediately admitted as a State under the Constitution, recently formed and adopted by her people, and accepted by the House of Representatives.

---

[1]   Misspelled in the 1860 Greeley text as *cotemporaneous*.

12. That, while providing revenue for the support of the General Government by duties upon imports, sound policy requires such an adjustment of these imposts as to encourage the development of the industrial interests of the whole country; and we commend that policy of national exchanges which secures to the working men liberal wages, to agriculture remunerating prices, to mechanics and manufacturers an adequate reward for their skill, labor, and enterprise, and to the nation commercial prosperity and independence.

13. That we protest against any sale or alienation to others of the Public Lands held by actual settlers, and against any view of the Homestead policy which regards the settlers as paupers or suppliants for public bounty; and we demand the passage by Congress of the complete and satisfactory Homestead measure which has already passed the House.

14. That the Republican Party is opposed to any change in our Naturalization Laws or any State legislation by which the rights of citizenship hitherto accorded to immigrants from foreign lands shall be abridged or impaired; and in favor of giving a full and efficient protection to the rights of all classes of citizens, whether native or naturalized, both at home and abroad.

15. That appropriations by Congress for River and Harbor Improvements of a National character, required for the accommodation and security of an existing commerce, are authorized by the Constitution, and justified by the obligations of Government to protect the lives and property of its citizens.

16. That a Railroad to the Pacific Ocean is imperatively demanded by the interests of the whole country; that the Federal Government ought to render immediate and efficient aid in its construction; and that, as preliminary thereto, a daily Overland Mail should be promptly established.

17. Finally, having thus set forth our distinctive principles and views, we invite the cooperation of all citizens, however differing on other questions, who substantially agree with us in their affirmance and support.

New Selected Bibliography

The Text – The main text of *Vote Lincoln!* is restored and annotated from the original book by John Locke Scripps, published in 1860 as *Life of Abraham Lincoln* (Chicago: Chicago Press & Tribune, 1860). An edition at the Library of Congress served as the source.

The genesis of the original book is discussed in the introductions to two reprints: *The First Published Life of Abraham Lincoln,* Grace Locke Scripps Dyche,[1] editor (Detroit: Cranbrook Press, 1900); and *Life of Abraham Lincoln,* Roy Basler and Lloyd A. Dunlap, editors (Bloomington: Indiana University Press, 1961). The former reprints the edition published in 1860 by the Chicago *Press and Tribune*; the latter, by the New York *Tribune.* Both reprints, though, polish and modify their original texts, e.g., correcting typographical errors and modernizing format.

Lively background correspondence is in the Abraham Lincoln Papers at the Library of Congress. Mr. Lincoln's discussion with Mr. Scripps about his bleak childhood is also reported by the former's law partner, William Herndon, in the opening pages of his *Herndon's Lincoln* (Chicago: Belford, Clarke and Company, 1889).

Historical References – The "look and feel" of Mr. Lincoln's world is in Carl Sandburg's six-volume biography, *Abraham Lincoln, The Prairie Years* (New York: Harcourt, Brace & Co., 1926) and *Abraham Lincoln, The War Years* (New York: Harcourt, Brace & Co., 1939), which won the Pulitzer Prize for history in 1940. A one-volume version is *Abraham Lincoln, The Prairie Years and The War Years* (New York: Harcourt, Brace, 1974).

Also useful are Horace Greeley's *A Political Textbook for 1860* (New York: Tribune Association, 1860), a compendium of major documents and speeches; John H. Barrett's *Life of Abraham Lincoln* (New York: Moore, Wilstach, and Baldwin, 1865); John G. Nicolay's and John Hay's *Abraham Lincoln: A History* (New York: Century Company, 1896); and Ida Tarbell's two biographies of Mr. Lincoln (see below). Frederick Douglass's foray into Illinois politics in 1854 is described by Frederic May Holland in his *Frederick Douglass, the Colored Orator* (New York: Funk & Wagnalls, 1891).

Messrs. Nicolay and Hay, who were Mr. Lincoln's secretaries, also edited *Abraham Lincoln: Complete Works* (New York: The Century Company, 1894). The collection includes Mr. Lincoln's "Autobiography," a partial manuscript for this book; thoughts on the tariff; and an 1857 speech condemning sexual abuse of slaves. Nevertheless, the most authoritative version of the Lincoln-Douglas debates is that edited by Mr. Lincoln himself, *Political Debates be-*

---

[1]   Ms. Dyche was the daughter of John Locke Scripps.

tween Hon. Abraham Lincoln and Hon. Stephen A. Douglas in the Celebrated Campaign of 1858, in Illinois (Columbus, Ohio: Follett, Foster & Co., 1860). Mr. Lincoln deleted crowd noises, giving a glimpse of his personal reaction to the debates. Fifty years later, those crowd noises were restored by Edwin Erle Sparks in *The Lincoln-Douglas Debates of 1858* (Springfield: Illinois State Historical Society, 1908), which also reprints media reports.

A later discussion of the debates is Robert W. Johannsen's introduction to *The Lincoln-Douglas Debates* (New York: Oxford University Press, 1965). Other recent treatments of the Lincoln era include Ken Burns's and Geoffrey Ward's *The Civil War* (New York: Vintage Books, 1990, 1994), the companion tome to the celebrated PBS television series; David Herbert Donald's *Abraham Lincoln* (New York: Simon & Schuster, 1995); and Stephen B. Oates's *With Malice Toward None* (New York: HarperPerennial, 1994). A compact collection of documents is *Abraham Lincoln, Speeches and Writings* (New York: Library of America, 1989).

Recent scholarly works shed more light on industrial slavery in antebellum America. An example is Wilma A. Dunaway's *Slavery in the American Mountain South* (New York: Cambridge University Press, 2003). Frederick Douglass's warning of slavery's threat to white workers, e.g., Irish immigrants, is appended to his *My Bondage and My Freedom* (New York: Miller, Orton, and Mulligan, 1855).

Estimates of modern dollars, based on equivalents for year 2007, are extrapolated from data of the U.S. Bureau of Labor Statistics, and the U.S. Census Bureau's *Historical Statistics of the United States, Colonial Times to 1970* (Washington: Government Printing Office, 1975).

Illustrations – Archival sources of historic images include the Library of Congress and the National Archives. The National Park Service has modern pictures of Lincoln historical sites, e.g., his birthplace.

Older books also have useful images, including Ida Tarbell, *The Early Life of Abraham Lincoln* (New York: S.S. McClure, 1896) and *The Life of Abraham Lincoln* (New York: Lincoln History Society, 1907); Nathaniel Stephenson, *Abraham Lincoln and the Union* (New Haven: Yale University Press, 1921); Alexander K. McClure, *Abe Lincoln's Yarns and Stories* (New York: Henry Neil, 1901); Joseph Fort Newton, *Lincoln and Herndon* (Cedar Falls, Iowa: The Torch Press, 1910); William Herndon and Jesse W. Weik, *Abraham Lincoln: The True Story of a Great Life* (New York: D. Appleton & Co., 1895); Osbourne H. Oldroyd, *Lincoln's Campaign* (Chicago: Laird & Lee, 1896); De Witt C. Peters, *Pioneer life and frontier adventures* ... (Boston: Estes and Lauriat, 1880); and Theodore Ayrault Dodge, *A Birds-Eye View of Our Civil War* (New York: Houghton Mifflin, 1911).

New Index of Persons

A Note about John Locke Scripps

John Locke Scripps (1818-1866) was a longtime friend of Abraham Lincoln and a founder of what became the Chicago *Tribune*. During Mr. Lincoln's historic run for the presidency in 1860, the two friends collaborated on a bestselling campaign biography. (Mr. Lincoln wrote a condensed manuscript, and under his direction Mr. Scripps expanded it into a full-length book.)

Mr. Scripps was well qualified to be Mr. Lincoln's biographer and coauthor. Mr. Scripps was a fellow native of the American frontier, being born in 1818 in sparsely settled Missouri Territory. His father was a tanner and named his son for John Locke, the philosopher who inspired the American Revolution.

In 1821 Missouri became a slave State. However, a Methodist religious revival graced and transformed the Scripps clan. An uncle was a prominent minister; the father freed his slaves in an act of repentance; and in the 1830s the Scripps kindred moved to the Free State of Illinois (as had the Lincolns). There young John Locke Scripps graduated from McKendree College in 1844 and became a professor, lawyer, and news editor. In the 1850s he was a founding partner of a major newspaper, the Chicago *Press and Tribune*, which was later renamed the Chicago *Tribune*.

As early as the 1840s, John Locke Scripps was an antislavery activist and in 1854 began promoting the prospects of the then obscure Abraham Lincoln. In 1858, during Mr. Lincoln's uphill Senate race against the incumbent Stephen Douglas, Mr. Scripps supervised a highly innovative news team. His reporters used new "shorthand" recording techniques, express trains, and the telegraph to publish overnight transcripts of the Lincoln-Douglas debates. Their groundbreaking coverage was syndicated coast-to-coast and helped make Abraham Lincoln into a national figure.

Mr. Scripps was a grandson of the English immigrant William Scripps (1749-1823), who spawned a remarkable family of publishers. Successive generations established not only the Chicago *Tribune*, but the Scripps-Howard chain of newspapers, United Press International, the Detroit *News*, the Cleveland *Press*, and several regional chains. Philanthropic activities included the founding of Scripps College and the Scripps Institution of Oceanography in California.

CPSIA information can be obtained at www.ICGtesting.com
Printed in the USA
LVOW120841280113

317499LV00003B/350/P